CW00493189

This is a highly readable, matters and its positive in any educator that places heart of their curriculum staff need frequent and r learning and play. More than that, Alexia explains how to ensure that this time is mediated sensitively to best effect. It is a call to literally 'green' our practice.

JULIET ROBERTSON, AUTHOR OF
DIRTY TEACHING AND *MESSY MATHS*

I loved reading this book! Not only is it accessible and engaging, it offers support and challenge to educators in considering, and adopting, nature-based practice. It is an invitation to become part of a conversation; a movement, a culture shift, where we relearn to be *part* of nature – not *apart* from nature. Full of provocations, tips and examples, this book is sure to become an essential addition to the practitioner toolbox.

MAIRI FERRIS, THRIVE OUTDOORS FUND MANAGER,
INSPIRING SCOTLAND

Every child deserves a teacher who has read Alexia's latest book, and it couldn't come at a better time following the global experience of a pandemic. Bringing together her extensive understanding of research related to nature connection and nature-based learning, this enjoyable read is inspiring and practical; relevant for teachers across early years to secondary and for student teachers. The short case studies are invaluable and it comes with activities to help everyone take steps forward in nature-based learning.

DR LAUREN BOATH, SENIOR LECTURER IN SCIENCE
EDUCATION (PHYSICS), DIRECTOR OF INITIAL
TEACHER EDUCATION & UNDERGRADUATE,
UNIVERSITY OF GLASGOW

Drawing on her vast experience as a teacher, lecturer and mother, and as the daughter of a committed naturalist, Dr Barrable delivers expert advice on how we can help children cultivate a love for the natural world. Her key message is that we cannot connect to nature just by being in contact with it. She shows how empathy and compassion need to be nurtured whilst also referencing a range of published research that demonstrates the significance of an improved relationship with nature. It is the combination of tried and tested practical examples, linked to relevant academic research, that makes this book such a gem for educators and anyone interested in igniting and developing children's love of nature. A serious topic and a joyful read that any teacher would be grateful for.

DR DYLAN ADAMS, SENIOR LECTURER IN EDUCATION, CARDIFF METROPOLITAN UNIVERSITY

Alexia Barrable's timely book concisely takes us through the multitudinous benefits of regular contact with the natural world. The book is aimed at educators of children, but the content contains valuable lessons for us all. This is in the form of citing research on brain function and behaviour which illustrates why these benefits accrue but, just as importantly for teachers, there are many practical examples to show them how and why access to nature is vital, both inside and outside the classroom.

As a head teacher of 20 years, I learned much from this book as well as being reminded about how valuable nature-based learning is and how we ignore it at our peril. If every school adopted its practices in full, the education system would have little to worry about and we would have much less to worry about regarding the education system.

DR DAVID DIXON, EX-HEAD TEACHER,EDUCATION CONSULTANT, AUTHOR OF *LEADERSHIP FOR SUSTAINABILITY*

INDEPENDENT
THINKING
ON ...

NATURE-BASED LEARNING

Alexia Barrable

IMPROVING LEARNING AND WELL-BEING
BY TEACHING WITH NATURE IN MIND

ındependent
thinking press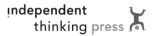

First published by

Independent Thinking Press
Crown Buildings, Bancyfelin, Carmarthen, Wales, SA33 5ND, UK
www.independentthinkingpress.com

and

Independent Thinking Press
PO Box 2223, Williston, VT 05495, USA
www.crownhousepublishing.com

Independent Thinking Press is an imprint of Crown House Publishing Ltd.

Edited by Ian Gilbert.

The Independent Thinking On … series is typeset in Azote, Buckwheat TC Sans,
Cormorant Garamond and Montserrat.

The Independent Thinking On … series cover style was designed by Tania Willis
www.taniawillis.com.

British Library Cataloguing-in-Publication Data
A catalogue entry for this book is available from the British Library.

Print ISBN 978-178135408-7
Mobi ISBN 978-178135412-4
ePub ISBN 978-178135413-1
ePDF ISBN 978-178135414-8

LCCN 2022935906

Printed and bound in the UK by
TJ Books Ltd, Padstow, Cornwall

MIX
Paper from
responsible sources
FSC® C013056

FOREWORD

Anyone with young children knows that a 'lovely walk in the countryside' is the worst thing you can do to engender a life-long love of nature in them. That mile-long hike to see the stunning waterfall/special tree/amazing view soon becomes a painful trudge accompanied by a regular chorus of 'Are we there yet?' and ends with at least one point of agreement – never again.

Then you wake up one morning and the sun is shining and the birds are singing and your optimism, like the sap in spring, is rising and off you go again. If only you stopped and realised that nature isn't something 'over there'. It's everywhere. If only you stopped and realised you can find as much beauty in an overgrown verge as you can in that stunning waterfall/special tree/amazing view. If only you kitted yourselves out for the hike but went as far as the muddy puddle within sight of the house and just stopped there. And played. For an hour.

A love of nature is a beautiful thing. Natural, if you like. But it is fragile. Nature is wonderful but it is also too cold and too hot and too wet and not muddy enough and hard to deal with and easy to hate. If the job of the adult is to bring out the love of nature in a child in a world of quick-fix media and shortening attention spans, then the job of the adult is to find the nature buttons to press. And while the teacher teaching outside will enjoy many benefits, this alone is no guarantee that you are helping that child grow up to love the natural world. As Principal Skinner explains to Bart Simpson as they prepare for a spot of astronomy out in the open one night, 'Ah, there's nothing more exciting than science. You get all the fun of sitting still, being quiet, writing down numbers, paying attention ... science has it all.'[1]

My own love of nature, birds especially, didn't come from being pushed out into the woods at the crack of sparrows. It started when my grandfather gave me a book about how to identify birds.[2] I still have it; both the book and the love. With the book as the key, the natural world opened up before me. No pushing was needed. This book by Dr Alexia Barrable is a key too. It is a simple, easy-to-read and easy-to-apply guide to helping develop a love of all things natural in all children. It's not only about taking them outside into nature – it's about bringing nature inside to them too. It's about learning *with* nature, not just *in* nature or *through* nature. It's about helping children become adults who will love, respect and care for the natural world at a time when the natural world is in trouble; man-made trouble.

We need this book like never before.

IAN GILBERT
SOMEWHERE IN CHESHIRE

---

1   *The Simpsons*, 'Bart's Comet', dir. Bob Anderson [TV series] (Gracie Films, 1989-present).

2   R. T. Peterson, G. Mountford and P. A. D. Hollum, *A Field Guide to the Birds of Britain and Europe* (London: Collins, 1974).

ACKNOWLEDGEMENTS

How do you thank a village? Words cannot express my gratitude towards the inspirational people who have kept the dream alive for me along the way: my colleagues, fellow researchers from around the globe who work in the field of children and nature – and especially Sam Friedman for her time and advice.

To my pupils, who fill me with hope about the next generation of teachers.

A big thank you to two very special mentors who keep opening doors: Professor Tim Croudace and Professor Divya Jindal-Snape.

This wouldn't have been possible without Ian and the team at Crown House, whose comments and guidance have been invaluable and to the point!

Finally, a big thank you to my family: Duncan, for his continued support and inspirational work with children outdoors; my two boys, Joe and Ollie, whose relationship with nature keeps evolving and deepening and keeps reminding me why this work is important for all children; my mum, who let me get muddy, play with fire and climb trees to my heart's delight; finally, to my dad, who inspired my love for the natural world and who is now 'the swift uplifting rush/Of quiet birds in circled flight'.[1]

---

1   Both Mary Elizabeth Frye (1905–2004) and Clare Harner (1909-1977) have claimed to be author of the poem 'Immortality'; its true authorship remains unknown.

CONTENTS

CONTENTS

FIRST THOUGHTS

As we navigate the multiple small and large challenges posed by the 21st century, including enormous ones such as the climate crisis and a global pandemic, many of us are looking for solutions in nature. Nature-based solutions, the sustainable use of natural processes and features to tackle societal challenges, are front and centre in our bid to restore balance and create a sustainable future. It is my conviction that in education, too, nature-based learning is one of the ways in which to creatively tackle some of the challenges we face, but also a way to future-proof our practice. The benefits of considering a turn towards nature-based education, whether it is on a small or incrementally larger scale, are numerous – both for humans, with regard to our well-being and ability to thrive, and for the planet. I propose that we invest in this symbiotic relationship – by fully understanding our place within nature, rather than apart from it – and bring nature back into all aspects of our own and our pupils' lives. In this book, I will put forward this argument by sharing the current state of evidence from the scientific literature and by putting it into scalable and practical contexts. Furthermore, by sharing examples of how others have put it into practice, as illustrated in the case studies provided throughout, I hope to inspire and facilitate this change for all. Start small and be brave!

A BIT ABOUT ME

It may sound like a bit of a cliché to start by saying that nature played a big part in my childhood – as it seems that every naturalist and nature lover starts their life story thus. However, in my case, the nature that surrounded my childhood games and first memories is largely urban nature. You see, I grew up in Athens in the 1980s – the capital with the lowest estimates of green area per person, with a mere 0.96m^2 for each adult and child according to the Organization for Economic Co-operation and Development. To put that into context, the World Health Organization recommends 9m^2 per person in order to support health and well-being.[1] And yet, nature was everywhere. My father was a naturalist and brought nature into our home in all its forms. We lived in a small flat for most of my childhood, but we had a gorgeous garden of potted plants on our balcony – I still remember growing tomatoes and peppers, and getting excited at the new daffodils breaking the soil in early spring. Actions speak louder than words, and I knew that my parents cared for nature in a very deep way; my dad rescued wildlife and nurtured it back to life. Our bathroom was, at different times, the temporary home of a recuperating common moorhen, a Eurasian owl with an injured wing, a corn crake that had been shot and a hedgehog hit by a car. More permanent residents of our home, when we eventually moved to a ground-floor flat with access to a garden, were two cats and a tortoise. Invariably, my brothers and I were interested in nature, but we also saw it as an integral part of our lives. It didn't exist as a separate place that we visited at weekends, but was in and around our home.

---

1   S. Karakasidis, WWF Greece introduces app mapping urban green areas, *Greece Is* (14 June 2016). Available at: https://www.greece-is.com/news/wwf-greece-introduces-app-mapping-urban-green-areas.

In my early teens I moved to England and was really taken by the accessibility of urban nature. Parks and commons, meadows and canals – I loved being able to explore and immerse myself in a different sort of natural landscape. My first teaching post was in London and it took me several years to start bringing nature into my practice. I remember no input into outdoor learning or any nature-based education at university; most of our training was on phonics, mathematical thinking, child development and curriculum. It was as I found my confidence as a teacher that I wanted to take my pupils into nature and bring nature into my classroom. I have 11 years of teaching experience in varied settings and across the primary age range. The more I became comfortable in my role, the more I tried to include nature in my practice. I started slowly, taking my reading group outdoors, then introduced some indoor gardening. I brought some pets (well, a snail farm) into my classroom and began to plan trips, purely so that my pupils could experience nature – meet it, play in it, start being part of it.

Ultimately, I came into academia with a desire to learn more; to try different things out, to see how things work. My research has been focused on nature connection in childhood and beyond, as well as the exploration of human–nature interactions. What is it about nature that promotes well-being? How can we support our children's tendency towards connection? The questions are endless and the more I learn, the more questions arise. This book brings some of my accumulated knowledge of practice and research into what I hope will be a useful primer to help you, the practitioner, to bring nature into your teaching.

WHAT IS NATURE?

Close your eyes for a moment. Take a deep breath and let your mind travel to the last natural space that you visited. What can you see, smell and hear? Where is this place? A forest? A meadow? A beach? Now, let us think about what nature means to you. What do you think of when you think of nature? Most of us tend to have a very clear idea of what is and what isn't nature; we often conceptualise nature as something removed from human influence – something different from us. In fact, in many people's minds there is a very clear dichotomy between nature and human. In research conducted in 1996, Claudia Mausner asked people to define what the term 'nature' meant to them.[2] Most participants described nature as something different and away from human influence, highlighting this separation that a lot of western people feel from the natural world. Nature was seen as pristine and unspoilt: a virgin rainforest, an untouched stream in the woods, an unspoilt beach with clean, crystal-clear waters. This is definitely one of the romanticised ways of viewing the natural world – as something separate and away from us. I don't want to get overly philosophical here. What I want us to do, as we embark on this journey towards nature-based education, is to work together to challenge this notion – challenge our view of nature as something remote, and come to a more balanced understanding of what nature really is. A happy side effect of this is that we are likely to become aware of nature everywhere we look, because it *is* everywhere we look!

---

2 C. Mausner, A kaleidoscope model: defining natural environments, *Journal of Environmental Psychology* 16(4) (1996): 335–348.

FINDING NATURE

For the next few days, I want you to look for nature wherever you are – walking in town, looking out of your window, when in a room. What is natural? Start from the understanding that we are part of nature – even if we often see ourselves as apart from it. This is, in fact, the essence of the idea of nature connection that my own research is based on and that I will be looking at in depth in upcoming chapters. The minute you start to notice nature, you realise it really is everywhere; from the bee that flies into your kitchen through an open window and the spider that lives behind your dresser (my dresser anyway), to the moss that covers part of your patio and the weeds that come out from between the cracks of paving stones. This shift in attention is key to changing our relationship to the natural world, but also to bringing nature into our teaching and learning – towards including the natural world in more of what we do in and out of the classroom. We find nature everywhere: in our homes, our gardens, in our cities and schools. Urban nature has been overlooked for a long time, and yet recent research suggests that it can have measurable positive effects on people's health and well-being.[3] Studies have reported benefits of engaging with urban nature on physical and psychological well-being, conservation behaviours and even improved executive functions in children, which are the set of cognitive processes that allow us to plan and execute complex actions, and attention.[4]

---

3 L. Taylor, A. K. Hahs and D. F. Hochuli, Wellbeing and urban living: nurtured by nature, *Urban Ecosystems* 21(1) (2017): 197–208.

4 A. R. Schutte, J. C. Torquati and H. L. Beattie, Impact of urban nature on executive functioning in early and middle childhood. *Environment and Behavior* 49(1) (2017): 3–30.

So, although most of us don't find ourselves with unlimited access to unspoilt natural spaces for our teaching and learning (though I am aware that some of you do – lucky you!), we all have natural features in playgrounds and neighbourhoods around our school; a grassy area, a few trees or some raised planters. In my first post in London, the playground consisted of a tarmacked area so small that breaktime was staggered. With the help of the parent–teacher association, we managed to add a variety of sturdy pots around one of the playground edges. This attracted a lot of interest from the children and was looked after by Year 4 and Year 5 classes. It also attracted wildlife, insects and pollinators, birds and sometimes small mammals and other animals (we soon noticed that at a certain time of year a load of 'two-headed frogs' appeared around our pots, so we had to – some of us reluctantly – cover reproduction in amphibians).

The tide is, however, changing – and in 2020 the 'greening' of school playgrounds became the principle aim of a £6.4 million campaign to improve children's well-being, learning and care for the environment.[5] Through adding natural areas to school grounds, the project aims to bring all children closer to nature and help everyone access the benefits of learning, playing and simply being close to the natural world. But you don't have to wait – you can start thinking about connecting with nature and its benefits as part of your teaching and learning today. A good starting point is to take an audit of what is accessible to you at your current setting. (See Appendix 1 for the audit form and instructions on how to use it.) Ideally, a few colleagues might join you in this exercise, ensuring that you don't

5 Nature Friendly Schools, New 'Nature Friendly Schools' will help to 'green' hundreds of school grounds and bring thousands of children closer to nature (1 February 2019). Available at: https://www.naturefriendlyschools.co.uk/new-project-will-help-green-hundreds-school-grounds-and-bring-children-closer-nature.

miss any spaces, but also so that you fully explore the possibilities of what your local nature can offer.

WHAT IS THIS BOOK ABOUT?

Nature-based education is not a set of activities. It is an ethos and a philosophy that brings nature to the forefront of our minds in all teaching and learning, and it nurtures a relationship between our pupils and the natural world. In this sense, nature-based education does not have to take place solely in natural spaces (although that is an important part of it too); instead, it is about learning with nature and about nature and includes a culture shift that enables the fostering of certain values and attributes, such as respect and empathy towards the natural world.

The term 'nature-based education' covers a huge array of diverse settings and contexts, programmes and experiences (for an extensive, though not exhaustive, list of what nature-based education is and can be, please see Appendix 1). Given their diversity and the varied contact with the natural world that each experience offers, their benefits also vary, both in quantity and quality. For example, spending all day in a forest nursery is likely to have very different benefits from taking part in animal-assisted learning. Equally, given that we work in different contexts and settings, we will all have varied access to the benefits described in this book. What I have attempted to do is to inspire and empower you to consider including nature in your work with children and young people. If you work in education, whether it be in formal or less formal settings, this book can offer you the information and motivation to start this culture shift and embed learning in, about and for nature in your practice. In less formal settings this may be easier, with fewer curricular and time constraints. However, it is in schools, especially primary schools, where this shift can have the most effect – on our children's ability to learn, their health and well-being, and their cognitive and social skills; all of which has been documented by a growing body of literature (shared in this book).

You may be surprised to find out that as a researcher in the field of nature-based education, I am often frustrated by the assertion that nature is good for children. I want to move away from that and other romantic notions which are taken as scripture. In all my work, I want to look at the evidence and scrutinise it – to take nothing as a given. For many years, the evidence was uncompelling and a lot of the studies done in this area were badly designed, with samples that were hard to generalise from or were biased from the outset. In the last decade or so, however, there is a body of research emerging that is bringing real rigour to why and how nature-based learning can be beneficial to children (and, as it happens, to adults and the planet too).

However, this is not an academic book; it is a book written for practitioners – for the people on the ground who bring children to nature and nature to the classroom. This cannot be done simply with a set of activities. Each chapter aims to explain the evidence so that you, the practitioner, can make decisions about how best to teach in, with and about the natural world. By knowing and questioning the evidence, and by understanding the mechanisms of action by which nature benefits a particular system, you can then make the right decisions and plan an activity that is optimised to support your learners' needs – be that well-being or improving attention. You can read this book from start to finish, if you'd like, or you can dip into a specific topic that interests you – improving behaviour, finding suitable inclusion strategies or enriching your learning environment. Overall, what I want you to do is leave the book lying on the staffroom coffee table. I want you to bring others along on this journey – to shape the culture of your setting beyond your own class or group. After all, this is what a culture shift is about. So, bring others with you and get ready for the ride!

TAKEAWAY POINTS

- Nature does not need to be an unspoilt paradise. There is nature everywhere (even indoors).

- Urban nature can have many positive effects.

- Directing our attention towards nature – simply noticing the nature around us – can be beneficial.

CHAPTER 1

EQUITY OF ACCESS – WHO IS NATURE FOR?

TACKLING INEQUALITIES

Stop for a minute and consider the issue of access to nature. Who has access more readily? Think about, for example, leafy neighbourhoods and parks. Consider who has access to privately owned cars and the time and resources to drive out of town in order to access natural spots. Finally – the simplest of all metrics – consider private green space; namely, gardens.

The truth is that one in eight British households has no access to a private green space at home. Those who don't have access are more likely to be members of an ethnic minority, while in England specifically, a Black person is four times more likely not to have a garden, covered patio or balcony than a White person. Different localities are also affected in different ways – you are less likely to have access to a garden if you live in London, where more than one in five households have no private outdoor space. Surprisingly, Scotland as a whole is not far off this statistic – no doubt being pushed up by urban areas. What is of interest is that, even when we account for socio-economic status and age, Black people are still less likely to have access to private green space. Finally, even access to public green spaces, such as parks, is limited for minority ethnic groups. To add to the inequality of access, those who have

11

their own private garden also tend to live closest to public parks. Still, as a country, the UK has relatively high access to public green spaces, especially when we include playing fields and playgrounds. The good news for Londoners is that despite the fact that they are less likely to have a garden, they live in a city with the easiest access to public parks. Having said that, population density means that certain parks in London, like Clapham Common, cater for a population of close to 50,000 people – while the average park across Great Britain serves about 2,000 people.[1]

Access to green spaces is important, especially when looked at from a developmental perspective. A longitudinal study from Scotland that looked at different access to nature – namely gardens and neighbourhood nature – found that children living in homes with gardens had better social, emotional and behavioural scores at age 6.[2] Neighbourhood green space was also associated with better social skills. Residential green space during one's childhood – namely gardens and balconies – has also been found to be associated with lower risk of psychiatric disorders in adolescence and adulthood.[3] At the same time, proximity to public green space has a similar association

1 Office for National Statistics, One in eight British households has no garden (14 May 2020). Available at: https://wwwons.govuk/economy/environmentalaccounts/articles/oneineightbritishhouseholdshasnogarden/2020-05-14.

2 E. A. Richardson, J. Pearce, N. K. Shortt and R. Mitchell, The role of public and private natural space in children's social, emotional and behavioural development in Scotland: a longitudinal study, *Environmental Research* 158 (2017): 729-736.

3 K. Engemann, C. B. Pedersen, L. Arge, C. Tsirogiannis, P. B. Mortensen and J. C. Svenning, Residential green space in childhood is associated with lower risk of psychiatric disorders from adolescence into adulthood, *Proceedings of the National Academy of Sciences* 116(11) (2019): 5188-5193.

with better mental and physical health.[4] We can certainly make a case for the importance of growing up with access to green spaces – whether these are private or public – and yet, it is clear there are great disparities between regions, socio-economic statuses and ethnicities; disparities that became even more obvious during the COVID-19 restrictions. Schools offer one way to address these and present an opportunity for greater equity in access. School grounds should be the first port of call in bridging this divide. Access to green school spaces – meaning playgrounds that are almost park-like with greenery and other natural elements, such as trees or hedges – is associated with improvements to physical and mental health.[5] Unfortunately, a lot of schools in the UK do not have the autonomy, time or funding to make radical changes to the playground environment, as local authorities tend to have oversight. However, even small changes, such as adding raised planters or potted plants, or ensuring that children have access to any natural areas already included within the perimeter of the school, but are sometimes out of bounds, can be a positive step in the right direction.

HEALTH AND WELL-BEING FOR ALL

Health and well-being are inextricable parts of quality education, and an implicit (and in many parts of the world, including Scotland, Wales and Northern Ireland, explicit) aim of what we do in schools. Nature-based education can be a strong ally in this, helping us to nurture physically and

4   D. Aggio, L. Smith, A. Fisher and M. Hamer, Mothers' perceived proximity to green space is associated with TV viewing time in children: the Growing Up in Scotland study, *Preventive Medicine* 70 (2015): 46-49.

5   J. C. Bikomeye, J. Balza and K. M. Beyer, The impact of schoolyard greening on children's physical activity and socioemotional health: a systematic review of experimental studies, *International Journal of Environmental Research and Public Health* 18(2) (2021): 535.

mentally healthy young people. This short section can be useful for practitioners who wish to undertake nature-based activities, for leaders who want an evidence-based approach to effective health and well-being practices, or to lay out a case for directing funding in their schools.

As evidence is mounting about the positive effects of nature on our health, access to nature becomes more than just a luxury – it is now a matter of necessity and equitable access to basic quality of life. A minimum of 2 hours in nature per week seems to be necessary for optimal health and well-being.[6] Being in nature impacts our immune system through different mechanisms: early contact with nature in childhood can help build a more robust immune system through exposure to germs that can help develop a measured immune response (also known as the hygiene hypothesis);[7] regular contact with particular types of green environments, such as conifer forests, has also been found to boost immune functions through exposure to phytoncides;[8] in a recent experimental study, researchers in Finland found that children who played in outdoor areas that were made more biodiverse (from gravel to planted green areas) showed improved immune markers in blood and skin.[9] Such biodiversity interventions may prove crucial for maintaining or improving the health of urban populations. Other associated benefits to health

6   M. P. White, I. Alcock, J. Grellier, B. W. Wheeler, T. Hartig, S. L. Warber et al., Spending at least 120 minutes a week in nature is associated with good health and wellbeing, *Scientific Reports* 9 (2019): 7730.

7   H. Okada, C. Kuhn, H. Feillet and J. F. Bach, The 'hygiene hypothesis' for autoimmune and allergic diseases: an update, *Clinical & Experimental Immunology* 160(1) (2010): 1-9.

8   Q. Li, Effect of forest bathing trips on human immune function, *Environmental Health and Preventive Medicine* 15(1) (2010): 9-17.

9   M. I. Roslund, R. Puhakka, M. Grönroos, N. Nurminen, S. Oikarinen, A. M. Gazali et al., Biodiversity intervention enhances immune regulation and health-associated commensal microbiota among daycare children. *Science Advances* 6(42) (2020): 2578.

linked to the outdoors when compared to indoor spaces – such as improved sleep,[10] better eye health[11] and higher physical activity[12] – make nature-based outdoor learning an effective way to boost health and well-being in all our pupils.

INDOOR NATURE

There are, of course, instances when the grounds of the school do not offer much contact with nature, especially in inner-city schools. All is not lost, however, as there are ways to start greening school playgrounds, or ensuring access to nearby nature – including applying for grants from organisations such as Learning Through Landscapes,[13] the Ernest Cook Trust[14] or Nature Friendly Schools[15] for equipment and training.

If all else fails, consider bringing some of nature indoors. Biophilic design includes the use of natural elements such as skylights for natural light, green or living walls, the presence of water such as springs or fountains, and natural materials such as wood and stone being used in a variety

---

10 L. A. Wood, M. M. Tomlinson, J. A. Pfeiffer, K. L. Walker, R. J. Keith, T. Smith et al., Time spent outdoors and sleep normality: a preliminary investigation, *Population Medicine* 3 (2021): 7.

11 S. Xiong, P. Sankaridurg, T. Naduvilath, J. Zang, H. Zou, J. Zhu et al., Time spent in outdoor activities in relation to myopia prevention and control: a meta-analysis and systematic review, *Acta Ophthalmologica* 95(6) (2017): 551-566.

12 P. S. Tandon, B. E. Saelens, C. Zhou and D. A. Christakis, A comparison of preschoolers' physical activity indoors versus outdoors at child care, *International Journal of Environmental Research and Public Health* 15(11) (2018): 2463.

13 See https://www.ltl.org.uk.

14 See https://ernestcooktrust.org.uk.

15 See https://www.naturefriendlyschools.co.uk.

of public and private spaces. Although biophilic design has been increasingly popular in the architecture of office spaces, hospitals and airports, schools have been largely left behind. Yet, when indoor naturescapes – i.e. natural environments with multiple natural elements within one setting – have been studied in education settings, they have been found to be effective in reducing stress, improving attention and boosting well-being and creativity.[16] The authors write: 'potentially promising leads were found on the associations between campus green space and improved quality of life, perceived restoration, lower outdoor temperature, and between indoor nature and improved indoor climate'. Additionally, air quality and levels of humidity and circulating carbon dioxide were all improved in classrooms that had a number of potted plants, or green/living walls. Even simply viewing nature through a window from inside the classroom is beneficial, and can improve mood, recovery from stress and mental fatigue. And if you are wondering how you will be able to implement this in your inner-city primary, fret not! Studies that have looked at the effect of whole-wall murals depicting natural scenes, such as forests, coastal views or waterfalls, were found to restore attention and ease mental fatigue (the study I've referenced here contains photos of murals, should you need inspiration!).[17] So, if no natural views are possible, consider the use of permanent whole-wall stickers or large posters of natural landscapes on one wall of the classroom.

---

16 N. van den Bogerd, S. C. Dijkstra, S. L. Koole, J. C. Seidell, R. de Vries and J. Maas, Nature in the indoor and outdoor study environment and secondary and tertiary education students' well-being, academic outcomes, and possible mediating pathways: a systematic review with recommendations for science and practice, *Health & Place* 66 (2020): 102403.

17 G. Felsten, Where to take a study break on the college campus: an attention restoration theory perspective, *Journal of Environmental Psychology* 29(1) (2009): 160-167.

ACTIVITY: CREATING A NATURE CORNER

Commonly seen in early years classrooms, nature tables or nature corners are actually a great idea to engage pupils with the natural world around them. However, nature corners, especially when they are co-created, do not have to be limited to preschool – they can be a great tool for bringing nature into the classroom at all stages of primary school. The nature corner can be a permanent place within the classroom where children can display all that they notice and admire about and from the natural world. The key to this ongoing, year-long activity is leaving it open to children to add to and curate. Interest sections and curiosity sections are very attractive – children can display things they have found to be interesting; this may include actual objects, photos or drawings of phenomena or items, books or other materials they have engaged with. The teacher's role is to share in the excitement and continue celebrating the items brought in (I once had a jar of snails brought into the classroom, promptly left open, resulting in many slimy escapees joining our class for the best part of a week). Use the children's natural curiosity to keep exploring, noting the changes in seasons and weather, asking questions and finding answers. The simple act of creating this space for nature within your room highlights that you, the teacher, value nature and share in its exploration. It also provides a provocation for further learning and can drive enquiry.

BROADENING ACCESS – THE POWER OF THE NATURE RESIDENTIAL

Sometimes it can be very hard to bring nature into the classroom, or to find regular opportunities to experience nearby nature. Yet, even in children who experience nature-based learning regularly, we should not underestimate the power that one-off experiences can have in changing their perspective on life. Nature residentials, including various types of outdoor adventure education and wilderness expeditions, have long been considered a great way to elicit positive changes in the lives of children and young people, including enhancing personal and social development. This is particularly the case for children who see themselves as lacking in social and personal skills; as I have seen in my own research when looking at nature residential outcomes, the biggest gains are always made with those starting with low levels already.[18]

However, a word of caution – or rather, a point to consider – when you plan such outdoor adventure experiences: although many studies have found that such wilderness excursions can have a positive effect on several fronts – such as improving resilience and a number of soft skills, and increasing children's motivation and engagement – we need to be aware that with no change to what we do when we return to school, that effect is likely to disappear.[19] If you are planning for your pupils to have such an experience, do not consider it over once they are back. You need

---

18 A. Barrable and D. Booth, Increasing nature connection in children: a mini review of interventions, *Frontiers in Psychology* 11(2020): 492.

19 R. A. Scrutton, Outdoor adventure education for children in Scotland: quantifying the benefits, *Journal of Adventure Education & Outdoor Learning* 15(2) (2015): 123-137.

to coherently and systematically build in the support to develop the skills the children have gained and offer translational avenues – opportunities for them to practise these skills – in their everyday and school lives. This is, of course, more challenging than compartmentalising the wilderness adventure and keeping it as a fond memory, but taking the extra step to integrate this experience with the rest of school life is likely to give enduring results. One of the ways to do this is by tracking the experience from before to after and beyond. Ask pupils to explicitly reflect on their expectations, their potential fears going into it, and any other feelings they may have before the start of the programme or excursion. It is common here to see many pupils, especially those who have very little prior experience of outdoor pursuits, to express disinterest; this is likely to be a defence mechanism, or a fear of the unknown. Give them as much information as possible about the practicalities of the experience – what will happen, what will be expected of them, and, where possible, give them a chance to be included in the planning. This should help allay their fears and may even spark some excitement.

Ideally, the wilderness residential will have some reflection time built in – time to personally, or in a group, think and process each day and set goals for the next. I have also found it useful to encourage pupils to keep a diary – this may be highly descriptive for some, simply recording the day's activities, or for others there may be a closer look at feelings. This can certainly help to make the residential a more transformative experience, both in the moment and later when looking back. Even the most basic and descriptive diary can certainly help with recall after the event. For pupils who are reluctant or unable to record feelings and experiences in this way, consider using technology, such as photography or video diaries. Alternatively, if you are present during activities, consider capturing comments on video – even a brief glimpse of an elated smile after a successful abseiling challenge can bring back memories later on.

From my experience, your pupils seeing you taking part in some of these experiences can also be life changing. I have a fear of heights and would not ordinarily choose to climb tall structures, let alone abseil down them. However, at one of the first residentials I led as a teacher, one of the activities involved just that. Perhaps sensing my discomfort, my pupils asked me to take part and I couldn't refuse. Watching me stepping out of my comfort zone, but also cheering and encouraging me, was perhaps one of the highlights of the trip; they saw me as a fallible human being who, just like them, had fears and felt anxious. They talked me through going up and cheered me through coming down. It was a bonding experience for all.

Unpacking the experience afterwards is an essential step to being able to coherently embed the new-found skills and attributes into daily school life once back from the wild. For many children it will seem like a dream, or they will perceive of that person in the wild as different to who they are in school. It is part of your goal to help them integrate the person they found in the wilderness into their self-image back at school. This shouldn't take a lot of time; consider it an investment as important as the original wilderness experience itself. See Appendix 2 for an example of the planning template for each pupil to do this on an individual level, as well as a broader template to achieve this on a class level.

CASE STUDY: FROM THE INNER CITY TO THE SCOTTISH HIGHLANDS

The loch is cold, and as he jumps into the water it takes his breath away. He bobs to the surface, buoyed by his life jacket, and looks around at his friends. They all have wide smiles on their faces – they look so alive. He grabs onto the rope and pulls himself towards the shore, buzzing. Adam is an 11-year-old that many of his teachers would describe as 'troubled'. He is in his last year at an inner-city primary school in Glasgow, where he is often late or fails to turn up to class. His home life offers little support and he lacks motivation to engage with school – he seems to feel that there is 'no point'.

Adam's school applied and received funding from the Outward Bound Trust and attended a five-day residential at their Loch Eil centre in the Highlands. The tailor-made programme included challenges for all in the wilderness. It was designed to transform the way the children look at themselves – making them feel in control and believing in their power to achieve.

Upon their return, the whole class has a discussion and each student completes a reflection exercise to identify highlights, achievements and breakthrough points of the trip. Adam talks a lot about the fear he felt when crossing a certain wire bridge – his feelings before, during and after. In a class discussion, he agrees with others when they say that often we are capable of more than we think, and that fear of failure and negative self-talk can keep us from trying. He commits to bringing an awareness to his fears when presented with a new task. Adam's teacher also commits to reminding him of the strength that he has. Adam writes his new motto on the front of his jotter.

Two months on, Adam seems more focused and has a new-found confidence. His teachers notice how he is more likely to come into school and even participate in lessons. He talks often of his experience with Outward Bound, which was all the more impactful for helping him connect with some of his classmates and teachers. When talking about the experience, Adam reveals the impact it has had on his life: 'I can do more than I ever thought I could! My instructors believed in me, and now I believe in myself too.'[20]

TAKEAWAY POINTS

- Everyone has a right to access nature, and, as teachers, we can lead more equitable access.

- It is not 'all or nothing' – some nature is better than no nature.

- Indoor nature can have a positive effect too.

- Research has shown that even short residential trips in natural environments can have long-term benefits for children and young people.

---

20 Adam's story and report are a composite of those by many of the children and young people who have participated in Outward Bound activities. You can read their own words here: https://www.outwardbound.org.uk/ hear-their-words-our-impact.

CHAPTER 2

BEHAVIOUR

THE CHALLENGE

There is little doubt that misbehaviour, ranging from small disruptive acts to verbal or physical abuse, is one of the biggest challenges for teachers and school leaders. Added to that, disruption in schooling and school routines – and additional pressures on mental health for staff and pupils – have only exacerbated the issue. Challenging behaviour is not only a great source of stress for teachers, often leading to burnout, but can also have an impact on outcomes for all pupils within the class.[1] A survey by UNISON, one of the biggest representative trade unions for teaching staff, reports that up to one in five members of staff have been a victim of violence in school, while a third have witnessed such attacks. The numbers are similar for verbal abuse and bullying – suggesting that the challenge is endemic.[2] Now, there is no magic bullet, and anyone who tries to sell you one is most likely lying. There are, however, combinations of recommendations that are backed by evidence, and used successfully in a number of schools. Most of these are proactive rather than reactive, focusing on building relationships, supporting pupils' needs and ensuring that the learning environment is optimised.[3] Contact with the natural world can help with all of the above.

---

1   Education Endowment Foundation, *Improving Behaviour in Schools: Guidance Report* (2019). Available at: https://educationendowmentfoundation.org.uk/education-evidence/guidance-reports/behaviour.

2   UNISON, *Bad Form: Behaviour in Schools, UNISON Survey* (2016). Available at: https://www.unison.org.uk/content/uploads/2016/06/Behaviour-in-Schools.pdf.

3   Education Endowment Foundation, *Improving Behaviour*.

FROM FIGHT OR FLIGHT

One of the biggest favours we can do our pupils when we step into the classroom is to bring with us an understanding of what happens on a physiological and psychological level when someone is under stress. In evolutionary terms, stress was designed to protect us from danger – from the hidden lion that would ambush us and have us for lunch. It is a normal response to situations where we are in danger – but it is often triggered in other, more benign situations, or in situations where we perceive we are in danger, even if we are not. Not all stress is bad; in fact, in certain situations it is to our advantage that our bodies prepare for fight, flight or freeze. When faced with imminent physical danger – of the aforementioned lion that is threatening to eat us up, for example – our body responds by producing adrenaline (as well as other hormones) – you know the feeling; our heart starts beating faster, our blood pressure increases and we breathe faster and more deeply. Our body is preparing for a fight or, maybe, if we think we can outrun the lion, for flight.

The third option is freezing, shutting down – playing dead; maybe the lion will leave us alone after all. Blood is redirected away from our extremities (clammy hands) and stomach (butterflies) to our major muscle groups, to support their imminent use. Our pupils dilate, our peripheral vision is drastically reduced – nothing else matters but us and the lion. In such a state, it is hard to think logically. It is hard to make long-term decisions, or to behave in a measured manner. The problem is, for some children, this stress response can be very easily evoked and certain environments, including the classroom, can trigger it. Moreover, once it is triggered, it can be hard to come back to a relaxed state – to achieve emotional regulation (a term we will touch upon a little later).

An important point to make here, especially in relation to education, schools and learning, is that no one has the capacity to learn when they are in fight or flight. Being worried, stressed or in a state of upset is not conducive to learning, building relationships or any of the desirable outcomes related to education. Whatever it is that you want to be achieving with your pupils, it will not be happening if they have adrenaline coursing through their veins, heart rate elevated, blood vessels constricting and redirecting blood into their major muscle groups and lungs in order to help them fight or flee. Nothing about this state – the stress response – is conducive to learning. And yet many of us, and many of our pupils, for a variety of reasons, will be in this state when coming into school.

TO REST AND DIGEST

Something magical happens when we find ourselves in a natural space, such as a forest or a beach. It doesn't happen immediately, but after a few minutes our heart and breathing rate slow down and our blood pressure stabilises. We release muscle tension and our body starts producing less cortisol in response to stress. On a basic neurological level, our sympathetic nervous system – by which we mean our fight or flight response, often activated during modern day-to-day living – takes a back seat. In its place, our parasympathetic system is activated. Now, our parasympathetic nervous system is what we often label our 'rest and digest' state.

This is crucial for maintaining our physical and mental health – and yet, often we find ourselves caught in a cycle of constant sympathetic response activation. And while being in nature can help us physically relax, it can also make us *feel* more relaxed. This parasympathetic response that brings us into the rest and digest state can be key to helping our pupils regulate their emotions. And nature can help us achieve it, improving behaviour. This state of relaxation can only be achieved in an environment where we feel safe; being in natural environments can help with that. There are other things we can do to induce this response, and we will be looking at them when we discuss nature connection later on. But for now, when considering spaces for learning, consider how nature can help bring about an optimal physiological state.

ACTIVITY: YOUR BRAIN ON NATURE

It is worth spending some time, especially with older children, explaining a little bit about what happens to us – to our bodies and brains – when we are in natural environments. You may want to share some of the science as described above, or use a video to illustrate some of these effects (my own 2018 TEDx talk[4] starts with a short explanation of what a dose of nature does to us). Of course, the activity would not be complete without some self-observation. Find a natural space close to the school and observe what happens to you when you sit quietly within that space. You can use objective measures, such as heart rate, or subjective measures – how do you feel when you are in that space? How relaxed are you, from 1 to 10? If you're not able to find such a space, use a natural soundscape (as described in the case study below) and, again, record the changes in mood and physiology.

---

4   A. Barrable, The 100 days that changed my life (and how they can change yours too) [video], TEDxLimassol (10 November 2018). Available at: https://www.ted.com/talks/alexia_barrable_the_100_days_that_changed_my_life_and_how_they_can_change_yours_too.

We are always more keen to engage in an activity when we can see for ourselves how it benefits us. Don't be scared to share with the children how our surroundings influence us; it can inform their future decisions and behaviours. You don't need to be in the wildest forest of the Amazon for this to happen (in fact, I imagine such a place may feel rather hostile and unsafe for someone with a western, urban upbringing). We now know from a variety of research projects that simply having flowers in a room with us can have an effect on our mood, making us feel instantly happier, as seen in a study at Rutgers University. In a multi-study research project, Professor Haviland-Jones measured pleasure and happiness in a variety of ways, including by looking at people's facial expressions, asking them about their emotions and measuring their social connection and responses to others. In all three studies reported, both men and women presented more positive emotion when given flowers, or in a room with flowers. The effect was not just transient either – even three days later, participants reported lasting effects.[5]

Other studies have looked at how the mere image of a flower can aid recovery after a stressful event. In this experimental study, which included functional magnetic resonance imaging as well as subjective measures (i.e. asking people how they felt), researchers at the Institute of Vegetable and Floriculture Science in Japan found that looking at a flower after a mildly psychologically stressful event could produce a marked reduction in negative emotion, blood pressure and cortisol release.[6] In other words, flowers can help us feel, but also actually *be*, less stressed.

5   J. Haviland-Jones, H. H. Rosario, P. Wilson and T. R. McGuire, An environmental approach to positive emotion: flowers, *Evolutionary Psychology* 3(1) (2005). DOI.10.1177/147470490500300109.

6   H. Mochizuki-Kawai, I. Matsuda and S. Mochizuki, Viewing a flower image provides automatic recovery effects after psychological stress, *Journal of Environmental Psychology* 70 (2020): 101445.

And there's more! The previous study examined how simply looking at an image helped us recover from stress, but in other studies, such as the one from Chiba University in Japan, we see that interaction with indoor plants can be even more powerful. In this well-designed study, researchers found that interacting with indoor plants (in this instance, transplanting them) can have physiological and psychological benefits. Participants reported feeling soothed and comfortable, while their physiological response showed reduced sympathetic activity and lower blood pressure.[7]

Looking at pictures of nature can create these psychological and physiological effects, as can interacting with indoor nature. Smelling flowers can have a similar effect, while touching natural surfaces, such as wood, can calm prefrontal cortex activity and induce parasympathetic activation, thereby inducing physiological relaxation when compared to surfaces like stainless steel or marble.[8]

Finally, consider another important sense: our hearing. Loud noises activate an area of the brain, the amygdala, which immediately triggers our stress response (we can imagine the antelope stampede we need to avoid). Modern schools, with their crowded and open-plan classrooms, have sound levels that average 72 decibels (dB), fluctuating between 35dB (the equivalent level of sound found in a library) while doing quiet work and 90dB (a noisy restaurant) while working in groups or other activi-

---

7   M. S. Lee, J. Lee, B. J. Park and Y. Miyazaki, Interaction with indoor plants may reduce psychological and physiological stress by suppressing autonomic nervous system activity in young adults: a randomized crossover study, *Journal of Physiological Anthropology* 34 (2015): 21.

8   H. Ikei, C. Song and Y. Miyazaki, Physiological effects of touching wood, *International Journal of Environmental Research and Public Health* 14(7) (2017): 801.

ties.[9] The impact of being exposed to such high levels of noise for several hours a day can be high, but also can have a clear effect on our stress levels – especially when it comes to some of our highly sensitive or neurodiverse pupils. Moreover, anthropogenic noise and urban noise, such as traffic noise, can increase children's levels of stress and agitation, making them more prone to misbehaviour, further raising sound levels and creating a vicious, and escalating, cycle of noise, stress and misbehaviour. Natural soundscapes, like the sound of the waves or the wind through a forest, can mitigate some of these effects, by inducing the rest and digest response, leading to more regulated behaviour and better learning. In the words of the authors of the study: 'Students indicated that anthropogenic sounds such as people shouting, playing and talking were quite frequent and unpleasant' while lower sound levels and natural soundscapes promoted 'acoustical comfort, acoustical calmness [and] acoustical satisfaction'.[10] Overall, they state that these can promote positive learning attitudes.

So, consider the smaller and bigger ways in which you can shape the learning environment. Think about your own classroom; its decorations, the furnishings. Think about the effect such an environment has on your learners (and, of course, you). What small changes can we make to create a more positive environment conducive to the rest, digest and learn state?

9   B. Shield and J. E. Dockrell, External and internal noise surveys of London primary schools, *Journal of the Acoustical Society of America* 115(2) (2004): 730-738.

10 Y. N. Chan, Y. S. Choy, W. M. To and T. M. Lai, Influence of classroom soundscape on learning attitude, *International Journal of Instruction* 14(3) (2021): 341-358 at 341.

CASE STUDY: WORKING IN THE RAINFOREST

Ms Adamu teaches Year 3 at an inner-city primary in the West Midlands. Her class is large, with 33 pupils, and overlooks the school playground on one side and a busy road on the other. Noise levels in the class – both from external sources (such as other children on break and traffic) as well as from the children – can be very high, and behaviour fluctuates with them.

When children engage in individual, quiet work in maths, Ms Adamu uses a track of nature sounds of a forest river to play in the background. For literacy, Ms Adamu uses a track of birdsong. Although it does not mask the sound of traffic, it tends to help children to concentrate and stay focused on their work. Children know and expect the natural soundscape, and often request it at other times too – like during quiet reading, or golden time.

WILD TEACHING

Of course, the best way to harness the support of nature on behaviour is to take your class outdoors!

> Children cannot bounce off the walls if we take away the walls.[11]
>
> **ERIN KENNY**

> It's a wondrous thing how the wild calms the child.
>
> **UNKNOWN**

These two quotes are often cited when talking about outdoor learning. I'm a little uncomfortable about them both, although I find it hard to pinpoint why. I guess there is something about them that problematises childhood, which suggests that the child is something to be fixed or tamed – still, there is merit in these observations. In reality, the expectations that we have, even of young children, can be extremely high and outside what is developmentally appropriate; sitting still for hours on end and limiting interactions with their peers is what is expected in a class environment. Going outside allows the child to be in her natural environment – an environment that is developmentally appropriate, full of wonder and movement, interaction and solitude. Behaviour expectations in the outdoors are different, that is true. But on top of that, natural environments activate our parasympathetic system, bringing us all into a much more balanced psychological state.

---

11 See https://cedarsongway.org/.

Finding natural spaces within the grounds to take our teaching and learning outdoors supports positive behaviour, which can then follow us when we go back inside. A study of 11-year-olds that compared a group who participated in a forest-school education versus one in a traditional school environment, found that those in the forest-school group had significantly higher positive change in a variety of areas, including better mood, higher energy levels, and reduced stress and anger.[12] On top of that, those that were initially assessed as having poor behaviour saw the biggest positive change on behavioural measures. This is supported by a lot of anecdotal evidence from those of us who have worked with children and young adults in outdoor environments – as above, 'the wild calms the child'.

EMOTIONAL REGULATION

One of the skills children develop as they grow up is their ability to control their emotions. The skill of emotional regulation, or emotion-related self-regulation, is one that develops slowly and is dependent on various processes, including executive function, directing one's attention and effortful control. It is no wonder that young children, aged around 2–3, find it very hard to regulate their emotions and succumb to tantrums (you'll know it when you see it). Self-regulation is not only important when it comes to behaviour, but higher levels of self-regulation in children predict better outcomes in a variety of areas. These include

---

12 J. Roe and P. Aspinall, The restorative outcomes of forest school and conventional school in young people with good and poor behaviour, *Urban Forestry & Urban Greening* 10(3) (2011): 205-212.

academic attainment, more years of staying in full-time education and better relationships.[13]

Caregivers, teachers included, are a key element of this process and, again, in the early years most children will rely on their caregiver to go through co-regulation with them. In this process the adult, who has mastered their own emotional regulation, is able to safely guide the child through the storm of big emotions and out the other side. By recognising and naming the child's emotion ('I can see you are upset') to modelling and giving them tools to cope ('Let's take a few breaths together'), the child learns to accept and appropriately respond to emotions that can be so big that they are overwhelming. My own first experience of co-regulation was a baptism by fire. I had already been teaching for three years, but had not yet encountered a child who could so readily run for it. Ian went into fight, flight or freeze very quickly, although usually it was flight that took place. He would take off from the classroom so quickly that I would often lose him. As he was only 8, I would follow him out into the playground and look for him while my teaching assistant stayed with the rest of the class. I would often find him hidden under a bush, where we would both sit while our hearts went from racing to beating slowly, and our breathing returned back to normal. Once he calmed down, which could take anything between 2 and 15 minutes, we would return back to class more able to take on the challenges.

While this process of regulation and co-regulation is important and cannot be short-circuited, we now also know that certain environments can support the process of building self-regulation skills. The findings from a large

13 R. F. Baumeister, K. P. Leith, M. Muraven and E. Bratslavsky, Self-regulation as a key to success in life. In D. Pushkar, W. M. Bukowski, A. E. Schwartzman, D. M. Stack and D. R. White (eds), *Improving Competence Across the Lifespan* (Boston, MA: Springer, 2002), pp. 117–132.

meta-analysis (a study of all studies on a particular topic) suggest that nature contact can be a used as a promising tool in stimulating children's self-regulation.[14] The authors take it a step further and suggest that regular nature contact may even prevent future psychopathology.

But even looking away from cumulative nature exposure during childhood, going outside and into nature can promote self-regulation in the moment. Studies that looked at children's exposure to various natural environments and regulatory behaviours found beneficial effects of short-term exposure to natural images on lower order self-regulation – for example, being able to control one's impulses;[15] what this looks like in the real world is children who are able to meet behaviour expectations by being able to control impulsive behaviour. More sustained contact with real nature has been found to have an effect on mood and cognitive aspects of self-regulation too.

RISKY PLAY
(OR THRILLS AND SPILLS)

It may sound surprising, even counter-intuitive, but one of the best ways to develop the precious self-regulation skills children need is through risky play, and nature-based risky play is ideal. It sets the scene for the decision-making processes, the inhibition of impulsive behaviour and the basic weighing up of risk and reward. First of all, we should clarify the difference between what is a risk and what is a

---

14 J. Weeland, M. A. Moens, F. Beute, M. Assink, J. P. Staaks, and G. Overbeek, A dose of nature: two three-level meta-analyses of the beneficial effects of exposure to nature on children's self-regulation, *Journal of Environmental Psychology* 65 (2019): 101326.

15 F. Beute, and Y. A. W. De Kort, Natural resistance: exposure to nature and self-regulation, mood, and physiology after ego-depletion, *Journal of Environmental Psychology* 40 (2014): 167–178.

hazard. It is often the case that we use the words inter-changeably, but it is useful to understand the distinctions. Hazards are generally factors that have the potential to cause injury, for example an eye-level branch in a tree which has the potential to injure a child as they go past. Risk, on the other hand, is the likelihood of a child getting harmed, and the extent of the potential injury. As you can understand, risk fluctuates depending on the child's age, competence, skills and awareness. The adult's job here is to help children recognise these hazards and assess and manage the risk. In addition, the adults should also be able to help children understand the potential benefits of engaging with an activity, despite potential hazards, and taking steps to minimise the risk.

Risky play comes in many guises, although a lot of them are near-extinct in our children's overprotected existence. Ellen Sandseter, one of the most prominent researchers in the area of nature-based risky play, talks of the power of risky play to teach children risk assessment and mastering risk situations. She has worked with risky play for years, and presents a typology of the six categories of risky play that children engage in:[16]

1 **Great height:** Think about climbing (trees, climbing frames or even steep slopes) and jumping from such heights. This act of jumping is an act of losing control – it is an exhilarating experience of relinquishing control as you fall/jump off and hope that landing will not be too painful. It encompasses a big element of risk assessment ('Is this height okay? What surface am I landing on?') that happens internally but is important as it builds skill and confidence in assessing risk. As a general rule, do not help children onto a high

---

16 E. B. Hansen Sandseter, Categorising risky play – how can we identify risk-taking in children's play? *European Early Childhood Education Research Journal* 15(2) (2007): 237-252.

object – they will have a better understanding of the risk and their own skills if they manage to climb themselves.

2 **Speed:** A lot of traditional playground equipment combines speed and height – think of swings or slides – and even more are just about the speed. Can you remember the exhilaration of going around the merry-go-round? Or rolling down a steep hill? Or using a scooter or a bike to speed a little out of your comfort zone? Anyone who has observed young children play (or remembers being a young child) is familiar with these behaviours, and many more that aim to increase that feeling of speed and, with it, the feeling of fear. Think of the 4-year-old that comes down the slide on her tummy, head first, the world whizzing past her as she screams with delight. Or the 8-year-old who jumps off the swing while it is at its highest point, hoping to land on his feet. Fear and exhilaration, risk assessment and careful calculation in one simple act.

3 **Playing with dangerous objects or tools:** Although not common in UK settings, in Norway, where Sandseter undertook this piece of research, children are allowed to freely use tools that have the potential to be dangerous. Carpentry benches with hammers, saws and nails, or knives can help promote children's fine motor skills, while also helping them to risk assess. It is important to have a proper introduction on how to correctly use these tools – not as toys, but for their intended purpose. It is also important to slowly build the skills needed and give children appropriate scaling options. For example, a very young child may not be able to use a knife safely but can use a vegetable peeler to learn the skill of whittling.

Supervision and ongoing discussion for risk assessment is key.

4 **Playing near dangerous elements:** This will sometimes incorporate great height, in the case of playing near drops or cliffs. The average UK school playground will not have access to such features, although the use of fire can be considered as one such element. Playing close to a burning fire pit or near a body of water needs to be something that is regularly assessed and discussed with the children so that they are aware of the potential for getting hurt. Having said that, such elements can be key in supporting self-regulation and impulse control.

5 **Rough-and-tumble play:** This is a feature we have in common with a lot of other mammal species – from chimpanzees to tigers; from dolphins to rats. This very special type of social play-wrestling is characterised by vigorous activities, such as swinging and chasing, playful collaboration and positive emotions. It shapes a host of social, cognitive and emotional behaviours not just in human children, but in the young of all the mammals that partake, helping children practise the useful skill of self-control, as well as building strong emotional bonds and promoting empathy and compassion. It is a key way in which young animals of all species learn to be members of a group – but it has risks. As rough-and-tumble play is a type of competition, where one individual 'attempts to gain advantage over another', there is the risk of escalation into more serious fighting. It is communication among participants, usually non-verbal, and closely reading each other's expressions and other non-verbal signals that help avoid escalation and, even when mishaps occur, help everyone return to safe

interactions.[17] This type of physical play is not readily allowed in most UK settings, for fear of escalation or accidents occurring. Yet, with some planning and clear boundary setting it could be used to enhance children's interaction, teaching them vital skills and ways to read others' signals. It is key to share with children the importance of observing and communicating – or as some settings put it, 'look and listen' and 'think and talk'. This is especially important when such play takes place outdoors, where conditions can be different each day.

6 **Play where a child can disappear or get lost:**
   Disappearing or hiding can be a thrilling experience for children of all ages, provided that they actually stay safe. So allowing them to experience getting lost within the confines of the school grounds can be exhilarating. Consider the use of dens, tents or other places where a child might be able to hide – and allow for this to happen during designated times. This is particularly important as children start craving autonomy both in the late toddler years (3–5) and later in primary school (9+). (More on supporting autonomy on page 50).

---

17 E. Palagi, G. M. Burghardt, B. Smuts, G. Cordoni, S. Dall'Olio, H. N. Fouts et al., Rough-and-tumble play as a window on animal communication, *Biological Reviews of the Cambridge Philosophical Society* 91(2) (2016): 311-327 at 321.

CASE STUDY: CREATING A RISKY PLAY AREA

Woodland Primary School is set in a medium-sized town, in a rural area in the north of England. The grounds are extensive but void of much excitement as they mainly consist of grassy playing fields. The practitioners for ages 4–7 are keen to consult with the children to help them shape the outdoor environment. After consultation, it is clear the children are keen to incorporate climbing into the outdoor space. (For a detailed example of how to meaningfully include pupil voice in the shaping of outdoor space, please check page 94.)

Given the limited budget, and the constraints of the space, they decide to bring in several potato boxes that have been donated by one of the parents. Potato boxes used in agriculture for storing and transporting fruit and vegetables tend to be solid and sturdy, come in many sizes and can withstand harsh weather conditions. Three large ones, reaching to a height of 1.5 metres when on their side, can be stationary and provide thrilling climbing and jumping experiences. Smaller ones of various sizes that are easier to move about can be used for stacking and stepping. Before the children are allowed to use them, there is a co-created risk assessment (see Appendix 4). The children recognise the hazard but are also excited by the risk and use the area often. The practitioners report very few accidents and, although risky, the children are able to use the space without putting themselves in danger. They are able to regulate their own behaviour, but also help, encourage and look after each other. Soon enough, children aged 7–11 are keen to use the space, and are permitted to do so twice a week, when the younger children are elsewhere. The space is used very differently by the older children, who also ask for loose planks and pallets to enhance the space. After further consultation they added a tool station on one side, where children could work on wood with nails, hammers and saws.

Overall, risky play – in natural environments, especially – can be a great way to build socio-emotional, physical and communication skills. It is also a key way to learn to regulate emotions – primarily their fear, anger, frustration and excitement. Through risky play, specifically with speed and heights, each child can choose to expose themselves to an appropriate level of fear and practise regulating it by remaining calm and facing that fear. During rough-and-tumble play, on the other hand, children get exposed to emotions such as anger and frustration, and need to overcome them in order for the game to continue. The balance needs to be found between fun and aggression in order to play and not hurt or upset the playmate.

ACTIVITY: ASSESSING RISK TOGETHER

How do we get better at something? Well, as the saying goes, practice makes perfect (though my old rowing coach would always correct me and say 'Perfect practice makes perfect'). It is the same with risk assessment and management; the more we allow our children to do it, the more competent they will get at it. The more we take that responsibility away from them, the less likely they are to engage in risk assessment themselves. Even in children as young as 3, risk assessment can be a team effort. With such young children, consider modelling the process – look at the space, or if it is a space that the children are very familiar with, consider asking them to close their eyes and imagine it. What risks are there? What potential is there for getting hurt? Consider the weather conditions too – even a tarmac playground can become slippery when wet or icy. How big is the risk – what is the worst-case scenario? How likely is it to happen? How can we reduce the risk? Additionally, it is important to start weighing in the benefits. What will we gain from engaging in this activity? What can we possibly learn? These are just as important to consider.

With older children this process can be done individually too, and then bring everyone together to summarise. Have a look at Appendix 4 for a sample form that can be used – either with children, or by the children themselves. Although official risk assessments may be needed at set time periods, you should make a habit of undertaking a risk assessment discussion every time you enter the space anew – conditions and natural variation can mean that the environment is different each time you visit (for example, rain or ice can make it slippery, new fungi can appear overnight, strong winds can make branches and trees unstable, etc.).[18]

---

18 Note: some schools may require additional or previous teacher risk assessment.

TAKEAWAY POINTS

- Natural environments have a physiological and psychological effect on us.

- Our parasympathetic nervous system can be activated when in contact with nature, making it a conducive environment for learning.

- Risky play can play a big role in teaching self-regulation and helping children become resilient.

CHAPTER 3

RELATIONSHIPS

It is not an exaggeration to say that relationships are at the heart of education, at all ages. As Sue Roffey expertly writes, 'positive relationships in schools are central to the well-being of both students and teachers and underpin an effective learning environment'.[1] A lot of the building of such relationships relies on daily interactions, and the cultivation of a deep feeling of mutual trust and respect. Moreover, building relationships doesn't happen overnight, or in just one setting within the school, but it is part of an ecological framework that exists throughout the school. One of the best ways to visualise it is perhaps as a Lego tower, where a myriad of interactions build and support the relationship.

There is no shortcut to building these relationships – and, as Jackie Beere says in her book *Independent Thinking on Teaching and Learning*, the easiest way is to simply 'love your pupils'.[2] Genuine interest cannot be faked, but then again most of us went into teaching because we like children and want to make a difference in their lives; the majority of the time, deep and true relationships form over the course of a year. There are things that can and do help in supporting strong relationships and a sense of belonging in a school (best described by others in books you can find in the Further Reading section on page 139). However, if we have learned anything so far from the science shared

1   S. Roffey, Introduction. In S. Roffey (ed.), *Positive Relationships: Evidence Based Practice Across the World* (Dordrecht: Springer, 2012), Chapter 9, p. 2.

2   J. Beere, *Independent Thinking on Teaching and Learning: Developing Independence and Resilience in All Teachers and Learners* (Carmarthen: Independent Thinking Press, 2020), p. 115.

in the first chapter of this book, it is that the environment around us, whether built or natural, has a distinct role to play. Our surroundings affect us in more ways than one, in physical and psychological ways. They affect our mood, our brain activity, our sense of safety or danger and, ultimately, affect the ways that we relate to one another; natural environments can have a positive impact, while certain types of man-made and urban environments can increase stress levels and agitation.

As described in more detail in the previous chapter, when entering natural spaces we can go from a fight or flight state to a more balanced state of rest and digest (and learn, I often add). This state in which our parasympathetic system is in charge, is a wonderfully receptive state for a lot of things to happen, including relationship building. So, for many children, going into a natural space means they feel safe, less threatened or hyper-aroused than in a classroom, and are therefore more able to connect to themselves, to others and to nature. Research also suggests that exposure to green space may increase prosocial behaviour among children and adolescents. The authors of a review of the topic state: 'The balance of evidence suggests that the development of prosocial behaviour may be associated with exposure to higher levels of nearby green space,' hinting at the role of green spaces in the development of these behaviours.[3] When we talk about prosocial behaviours, we usually refer to behaviours that are driven by the intention to help others and include a variety of actions, such as sharing, comforting and offering emotional support, offering physical support or helping someone, and cooperation towards a common goal. All these behaviours are a key part of child development and something that

---

3   I. G. N. E. Putra, T. Astell-Burt, D. P. Cliff, S. A. Vella, E. E. John and X. Feng, The relationship between green space and prosocial behaviour among children and adolescents: a systematic review, *Frontiers in Psychology* 11 (2020): 859.

we all aspire to with regard to our children: we want them to play a role in a harmonious society, to be helpful to others and able to share and collaborate. Moreover, such behaviours feed into positive relationships with others, and are also considered a psychological asset with impact on both the community and the individual, in the form of increased well-being.[4] Think of the warm glow we all get when we feel we have helped someone.

Further studies have linked prosocial behaviour to other favourable outcomes, including academic success and improved mental and physical health. (See Further Reading for the positive effects of prosocial behaviours.) There are many hypotheses as to how green spaces can promote prosocial behaviours, but there is not enough evidence to agree on just one. Some research suggests that there may be a critical period in a child's life for the development of prosocial behaviours, and that access to green spaces at that time is key to developing well. Others rely on the cognitive-boosting impact of natural spaces, as well as the restorative effect that green environments can offer. For me, an important factor, and one that we need to consider when planning learning outdoors, is certain pedagogical aspects of our practice when in nature.

---

4   L. B. Aknin, J. K. Hamlin and E. W. Dunn, Giving leads to happiness in young children, *PLoS ONE* 7(6) (2012): e39211. DOI:10.1371/journal.pone.0039211.

CASE STUDY: THE OUTDOOR NURTURE GROUP

Riverside Primary School is located in an urban area with a high percentage of children eligible for free school meals. It has a tarmac school playground at the front, but backs onto a wooded area and a canal. Within the school, there is a well-established nurture group for children aged 5–7 that has been running for several years. The two lead practitioners, Claire and Bryan, have a combined wealth of experience and consider the building and modelling of strong relationships one of the key roles of the nurture group.

The current group is made up of 12 children aged 5–7 and they have been together since the start of the year. The nurture group is housed in an additional building that is not attached to the school, and the group have to walk across the playground to get to it. It is early on in the autumn term and the children are keen to explore the fallen leaves around some of the trees in the corner of the playground. Claire, who is committed to child-led practice, spends time with them outside in the small wooded area at the back of the school. Claire and Bryan notice the sense of enthusiasm, positive energy and exploration that the children bring to these sessions, and decide to design a more permanent area that they can use outdoors. After a storm in early winter brings down a large tree, they ask the school grounds maintenance service to not dispose of it, but rather to cut it into sections that can then be used as stools.

Bryan, who is developing an interest in outdoor learning, goes on a forest-school course and learns how to string a tarp for shelter and light a fire. The nurture group meets outdoors on most days of the year, when the weather permits, with a focus on the building of relationships between all members and with the natural world. Claire and Bryan note how calm the children can be when outdoors, and how they work together beautifully in that space. Collaboration comes more easily to them in that natural landscape and turn-taking for the use of tools and around the fire becomes the norm. Moreover, the children look forward to spending time outdoors, and start looking after the immediate surroundings of their outdoor nurture space.

As is important with nurture groups, the routines of the forest are predictable but also responsive. Claire is keen to bring rituals to support children's development and transition, and the preparation of special foods on the fire becomes an important part of the nurture practice. At the end of each term, a special feast of hot chocolate and pancakes on the fire punctuates the transition into the holidays.

NATURE PEDAGOGY

It is not too much of a generalisation to say that as important as the surroundings and context can be for supporting all the outcomes that we want, pedagogical aspects of our practice are just as important, and sometimes more so. All aspects of pedagogical practice – from behaviour and time management, to questioning and the type of activities we undertake – usually sit on a spectrum. On one side of the spectrum we have teacher-led and very structured, while on the other we have child-led and unstructured.

Teacher-led and structured ⟷ Child-led and unstructured

Most of us, as practitioners, have a comfort zone some-where on that spectrum; I call this the Goldilocks zone – a term borrowed from astronomy (which borrowed it from the fairy tale, of course), where it describes the habitable zone in relation to the Sun, where just the right conditions exist for life to flourish. Similarly, the Goldilocks zone is our comfort zone in relation to pedagogical practice, where we feel just right. For some of us that zone is quite wide – we have more flexibility to move across the spectrum to meet the needs of different pupils, classes, ages and spaces. Others have a narrow scope and tend to prefer a certain side of the spectrum. Our Goldilocks zone is influenced by our training, our own experiences as pupils, the school we are in, the class we have and, a lot of the time, the activity we are undertaking and the space we are in. A good range is probably a sign of a good teacher – being able to shape our own teaching to fit the occasion.

Nature pedagogy, or the pedagogical practice we use in natural environments, tends to sit on the right of the spec-trum above, being more child-led and a little less structured (although I will discuss the idea of structure further on and challenge some of what is often believed about structure and autonomy). Behaviour management tends to be less limiting, with children allowed to move and talk freely in the bigger space. Time management tends to be looser – allowing for children to take their time over activities and even get bored. There is more exploration in the learning and less prescription. There is evidence to suggest that this type of approach can support a child's three basic needs: autonomy, competence and relatedness.[5]

NEEDS-SUPPORTIVE PEDAGOGY

When we think about a child's needs, many of us think back to our lectures on Maslow. Indeed, that pyramid image – starting with our physiological needs and moving onto transcendence – often in rainbow colours, is imprinted on every education student's brain early on in our training. (It also turns out that it wasn't even created by Maslow himself.[6]) An alternative theory – self-determination theory (SDT) – examines motivation and well-being in relation to our three basic psychological needs. These are, as mentioned above, the need to feel autonomous, to feel competent and to feel like we belong. SDT is very much the dominant motivation theory in psychology these days – and has a big body of research to back it up.[7] Contrary to Maslow's theory, in SDT the needs are not hierarchically ordered but are equally weighted. Moreover, supporting one of those needs tends to support the growth of the others too. Let's have a look at some examples. (Previous

5   A. Barrable and A. Arvanitis, Flourishing in the forest: looking at forest school through a self-determination theory lens, *Journal of Outdoor and Environmental Education* 22(1) (2019): 39-55.

6   T. Bridgman, S. Cummings and J. Ballard, Who built Maslow's pyramid? A history of the creation of management studies' most famous symbol and its implications for management education, *Academy of Management Learning & Education* 18(1) (2019): 81-98.

7   R. M. Ryan and E. L. Deci, *Self-Determination Theory: Basic Psychological Needs in Motivation, Development, and Wellness* (New York: Guildford Press, 2017).

research has suggested that natural learning environments are ideal for supporting these needs in children.[8])

SUPPORTING AUTONOMY

Pupil autonomy, sometimes also referred to as pupil agency, is about acting with full volition – having a choice as to how to behave, what activity to undertake and how to go about a task. However, to be truly autonomous we also need to take into account the space we find ourselves in – our actions need to be coherent with the self (and what we want) but also with the social context. When we think about autonomy in young children it is important that the socialising agent, in this instance the teacher, is actively supportive of the child's need to lead the self. Autonomy is a desirable goal not only because it promotes well-being, but it is also linked to other positive outcomes, including better attainment, higher motivation and, in teenagers, staying in education longer (avoiding dropout). It is also highly correlated with positive relationships and a sense of belonging, as by supporting one psychological need we are nurturing the other two as well.

In a classroom there are many evidence-based approaches by which to support autonomy, and these can broadly be placed into three categories: organisational, procedural and cognitive autonomy support.[9] By allowing children to have some say in classroom management issues and routines, we offer organisational support. Procedural autonomy support is often manifested when we offer pupils the chance to choose how they can engage with an activity, or what medium to use to bring a task to comple-

---

8 Barrable and Arvanitis, *Flourishing*.
9 C. R. Stefanou, K. C. Perencevich, M. DiCintio and J. C. Turner (2004). Supporting autonomy in the classroom: ways teachers encourage student decision making and ownership, *Educational Psychologist* 39(2): 97–110.

tion. Finally, cognitive support encourages the children to take ownership and drive their own learning forward, but can also include self- and peer-assessment and other practices.

These approaches can be and often are, of course, used outdoors too, but natural learning environments offer so many additional opportunities. Surprisingly, one of the ways to support autonomy in the outdoors is through a clear structure. Not to be confused with being strict, a clear structure is about setting strong boundaries from the start. That structure may be quite loose – in that the boundaries can be very different to what they would be indoors – but they need to be clearly articulated and understood by all. For example, one of the first tasks when in an outdoor space is to set the physical boundaries of where children can and cannot go. This is common practice in all settings, from forest school and beach school to outdoor learning on school grounds. In a classroom the boundaries for moving around and out of the space are very clear, but they are also very restrictive.

In order to support autonomy in the outdoor space, you still need to have clarity but can have fewer restrictions. For example, some practitioners will simply say 'You can go anywhere you want, as long as you let an adult know'. This is, of course, done after the joint risk assessment has taken place. Others will use a fence or natural boundary, while some allow children to go as far as they can while still having eye contact with the teacher (with children usually being shorter it means that if they can see you, most of the time you can see them too). Some practitioners will ask children to set their own boundary for that session and weather conditions, and will place a temporary marker at the edge by tying a coloured rope around certain trees, for example. That space then allows for autonomy and freedom of movement. The same goes for time management, risk taking and other aspects you would normally regulate in the classroom and the school grounds.

A key aspect of supporting children's autonomy outdoors is allowing for ownership of place. This is something we saw in the case study on Riverside Primary nurture group (page 46) – encouraging the children to feel that the place belongs to them, but that they also belong to the place. In practice this looks like encouraging children to name each feature of the space, placing signs that they make themselves, or making maps that denote their ownership. Additionally, consider having areas that are child-only, where adults need to keep out! This idea of a hiding and/or resting place, where the child is in charge of themselves, is very strong – and it is often seen in the design and construction of dens. A child's den, whether indoors or outdoors, exerts their autonomy and ownership of that particular space. Being able to hide and rest within it, alone or with friends, further embodies the control of that space and particular time. Given the little autonomy our children tend to have these days, and lack of control over their space and time, it is quite a radical affordance of nature-based education for children, and fundamentally supports their basic psychological needs.

CASE STUDY: THE EARLY YEARS OUTDOOR SPACE

Little People Nursery is a small private nursery in an urban location. They have a large indoor provision and have recently tried to shape the small outdoor space they have. As it is, the space is about 12m^2 and currently covered in patchy grass. It also tends to collect water in puddles when it rains. The staff decide to add a mud kitchen at one end and use the other end as a raised garden bed where the children will grow vegetables that can be harvested and used in cooking. There is a shed that is used for storage of loose parts too.

The practitioners are keen to support the burgeoning autonomy of the 'rising twos' – these 2-year-olds are developmentally ready to start making their own decisions as to where they want to be and what activities they want to undertake. One of the easiest ways to do that, but with the most impact, is by creating the capacity for free flow between outdoor and indoor play. This is a fairly simple change that means children can decide where they want to be in the space, and how they want to spend their time. It also allows for children to choose to spend time on their own, or with others.

The second change the practitioners want to bring in relates to the idea of hiding and resting that was presented earlier. There is little space for a permanent structure such as a tree house in the small outdoor space, so they decide to bring in pop-up tents. These will be stored in the shed along with other loose parts and tools, which is accessible by the children. Children can decide to use them individually or with others, to read, rest or play, at any time of day. The pop-up tents are a huge success with the children and are often brought inside as well; some children are keen to add extensions onto them or write signs such as 'reading room' to denote ownership and purpose.

SUPPORTING COMPETENCE

The idea of competence describes the universal need we all have to master our surroundings, have some control within them and be effective in what we do. In this sense there is very much a balance between the task – what we are asked to do – especially when we are talking about education, and our level of expertise. Feeling competent comes from what is called optimal challenge, meaning that our skills and experience are very well matched with the task we need, or choose, to undertake. For many teachers within the classroom, this is what differentiation is about – being able to match the child's skills to the task.

Looking at it from the point of view of nature-based learning, there is more freedom to let the pupil explore their own capabilities and find a match for them within the setting. Going back a little to the topic of risk, as was examined in Chapter 1, risky play gives the child the opportunity to find the desired level; to stretch but not overstretch themselves in order to feel competent and effective. This is very much related to the zone of proximal development as outlined by famous pedagogical theorist Lev Vygotsky, outlined in the following diagram:

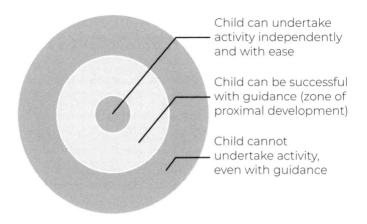

Child can undertake activity independently and with ease

Child can be successful with guidance (zone of proximal development)

Child cannot undertake activity, even with guidance

AN ILLUSTRATION OF THE ZONE OF PROXIMAL DEVELOPMENT

To further support competence in outdoor settings, it is important to consider the type of feedback we provide, especially when we are dealing with risky play. Staying away from feedback that is alarming and of no use (for example, 'Be careful' or 'You will fall'), the teacher here can instead try to offer directional and informative feedback that further builds the child's skills to undertake an activity. Think, for example, about a child climbing a tree – by giving personalised and incremental informational feedback (for example, 'Look at the branch on your right. Try it out – do you think it can hold your weight, or is it a dead branch?'), we allow the child to experience a high degree of autonomy on the one hand, and to acquire new skills and feel competent on the other.

SUPPORTING RELATEDNESS (OR A SENSE OF BELONGING)

To satisfy the need for relatedness is broadly to feel connected to others. This positive sense of connectedness includes being cared for, but also caring for others – it is, therefore, very much reciprocal. When we put it into an educational setting it is very much about the learner feeling liked, valued and accepted, but also feeling like a valued and respected member of the group. As mentioned previously, this is all about positive relationships and natural settings are ideal to build such good rapport; one reason is that we can reach children who are usually reluctant or unable to open up in a traditional classroom. Children who have difficulty regulating in a classroom, who feel threatened or defensive, can quite often lower or even let their guard down when in an outdoors context.

This can be the case for children with emotional and behavioural difficulties, or even learning difficulties that preclude them from achieving in the classroom and, therefore, feeling fully comfortable. This happens in a variety of ways, initially on a physical level as the sympathetic nervous system takes a back seat, and the parasympathetic system of rest and digest takes over. It also relates to the fact that, as we discussed earlier, the expectations are different, the boundaries leave more space for autonomy and competence, and there are opportunities for collaborative learning and exploration that are not often found indoors. In fact, when teachers are asked about what they single out as the best opportunities afforded to children in the context of outdoor learning, they identify collaboration

– between pupils, staff and pupils, and pupils and the local community.[10]

A RELATIONSHIP WITH THE NATURAL WORLD – NATURE CONNECTION

One of the gifts we can give the children in our care is to support them in developing a positive relationship with the natural world. This feeling of nature connection has been studied quite widely in the last couple of decades, not least by myself, and we now know quite a lot about the benefits of being connected with the natural world, but also of the benefits to our planet. What does it mean to be connected to nature? Well, the term describes a positive relationship with the natural world. This tends to be a life-long relationship, nurtured in early childhood and lasting into adulthood, although recent research has indicated a dip during the teenage years (this will not come as a surprise to many parents to adolescents).[11] This feeling of being a part of the natural world, rather than apart from it, as with any relationship, takes time to nurture. We now know that people who are highly nature-connected tend to be happier and have higher levels of general well-being, as well as, more specifically, feeling greater meaning in their lives.[12] They are more likely to experience vitality, and

---

10 E. Fägerstam, High school teachers' experience of the educational potential of outdoor teaching and learning, *Journal of Adventure Education & Outdoor Learning* 14(1) (2014): 56-81.

11 M. Richardson, A. Hunt, J. Hinds, R. Bragg, D. Fido, D. Petronzi and M. White, A measure of nature connectedness for children and adults: validation, performance, and insights, *Sustainability* 11(12) (2019): 3250.

12 Barrable and Booth, Increasing nature.

have greater acceptance of self, including their physical appearance.

Aside from the benefits to the individual, feeling connected to the natural world means that we are more likely to care for it – nature connection is positively associated with pro-environmental attitudes and behaviours like recycling, not littering and saving electricity. It has also been linked to our feelings of belonging in relation to other humans, our communities (social connection) and to promote prosocial behaviours.[13] This seems like something we should aspire to, for all our children, and encourage them to cultivate.

WAYS TO CONNECT WITH THE NATURAL WORLD

For a very long time, education has shown little interest in promoting or maintaining children's connection to the natural world. As the benefits of such a connection have become more widely researched and more widely known, interest has been stirred. At the same time, as the mental health crisis on the one hand and the climate crisis on the other have intensified and present a huge threat to our own and the planet's well-being, we have started reconsidering our relationship to nature. Even then, most programmes aspiring to bring children closer to nature within education have focused on two main aspects: contact and knowledge. This may largely be a pragmatic decision – after all, traditional educational institutions have always focused on knowledge to the exclusion of many other forms of experience. However, as we learn more about how a relationship to nature is cultivated, grows and bears fruit, it is becoming clearer (though it is also unsur-

13 Putra et al., The relationship between green space and prosocial behaviour.

prising) that it takes more than contact and knowledge to love something.

When I talk about nature connection to various audiences, I often say that just as we do not connect with people by riding on a busy bus, we cannot connect to nature just by being in contact with it. We connect to people through getting to know them, caring for them and being cared for by them, by having fun together, by having new experiences. Think of a first date, for example – what would you like to do? It is the same with nature: there is more than mere contact that is needed for us to build that relationship with it.

Researchers from the University of Derby have found that there are several pathways to nature connection; namely emotion, compassion, meaning and beauty.[14] Other research has found that mindfulness – being in nature and focusing your awareness on the present moment, your thoughts, feelings and sensations – can also enhance nature connection in children and adults (see the case study on page 68).

Bringing a lot of complex research together to present a simple plan on how to nurture nature connection in children is not easy, but here are some ways, supported by the science, that can be brought into school life. (I have also added some more specific activities – some ideas to get you started – but these are by no means exhaustive.)

---

14 R. Lumber, M. Richardson and D. Sheffield, Beyond knowing nature: contact, emotion, compassion, meaning, and beauty are pathways to nature connection, *PLoS ONE* 12(5) (2017). DOI:10.1371/journal.pone.0177186.

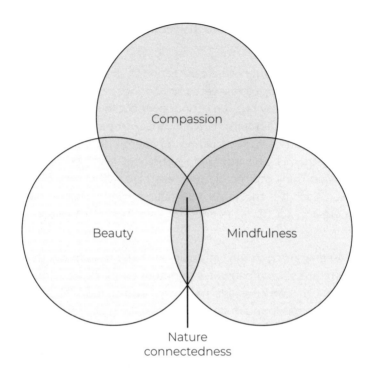

Compassion

Beauty

Mindfulness

Nature
connectedness

SUSTAINED CONTACT WITH NATURAL ENVIRONMENTS[15]

REGULAR CONTACT WITH THE NATURAL WORLD

The key here is to think about quality, not quantity. It is not necessarily about spending hours 'doing outdoor learning', but about potentially shorter but more targeted sessions; about the way the children start engaging with the nature around them. These can touch upon some of the themes below, or can simply be focused on free play and supporting autonomy. Get to know a particular place

---

15 A. Barrable, Refocusing environmental education in the early years: a brief introduction to a pedagogy for connection, *Education Sciences* 9(1) (2019): 61.

(read back to the earlier parts about supporting autonomy on page 50) – let children map their area out, organise it as they wish and name each space within the area.

Consider setting up collaborative tasks where children need to work together, or look at the following activity which brings both children and nature together. It can be used regularly, or you can encourage children to return to the object of their first encounter again and again for repeat visits and a closer relationship.

ACTIVITY: GETTING TO KNOW YOU

This is a fun activity, and one that won't take long, but will help the children connect to the natural features of your space, and to each other. Children are paired up (there is a real dynamic to the process of pairing up – you know your class – consider whether it is better to pair them up yourself, or whether you are happy for each to find a partner). One partner is chosen at first to close their eyes – I have in the past used sleep masks as blindfolds, collected over many years from airline travel and friends and family, or children can simply shut their eyes tightly. The other person is the guide. The guide chooses a natural object from a certain pre-arranged area: this is usually a tree, a rock or a bush. They gently guide the blindfolded person to that object, ensuring that they alert them to any potential dangers on the way; fallen branches, dips in the ground, brambles to get tangled in. When giving instructions, you need to emphasise the vulnerability of the blindfolded person, and how they are putting their trust in their guide to be kept safe. When they reach the object, they have a few minutes to get to know it. Touch it, smell it, try and get a full picture of it – what does it feel like? What does it smell like? How big is it? When time is up, the pair walk back to the starting point. The blindfolded person opens their eyes and has to guess, or rather work out, which is the object they have just been acquainted with.

There are ways to make the challenge harder – you can discuss this with the children; namely, the guide can take their charge on a more circuitous route to try and confuse them. This is fine, too. However, ensure that you take some time after the exercise has taken place to also discuss how the blindfolded person feels – this is an exercise in empathy for your learners. It is a very vulnerable position to be in, and the guide needs to put themselves in the position of the other person and anticipate what might cause them worry, or even hurt them. In round two, the roles are reversed – each person gets to experience the other role.

Taking the exercise a few steps further, you can ask the children to draw the object of their attention even before they see it, simply from having used their other senses to explore it. You can ask them to name it, to write a poem about it … you get the idea! The point is that this can be the start of a longer-term, ongoing relationship with a natural object in the natural space they visit regularly. It is a chance to watch the impact of season changes on that object and to observe how weather affects it.

ENGAGING WITH NATURE'S BEAUTY

Nature is everywhere, and, once you start noticing, its beauty is also everywhere. A lot of our existence is about where we choose to focus our attention – when we focus on one thing it is then easier to see it, and we see it everywhere. This is very much the case with beauty in nature – we can train ourselves to notice it. One way to do this is simply by sharing these moments with others – spending a few minutes at the start or end of the lesson to do so. Another way is to keep some sort of journal; this was what researchers at the University of Derby did – participants were to notice and note down three good things in nature each day, for five days. There was another group who had to note factual things (a control group, as it is called in experimental designs). The group who noted the good things – which were mostly about nature's beauty – saw a marked improvement in their sense of connection with the natural world.[16]

Technology can help. Many teachers I have spoken to who are passionate about nature-based learning and connection to nature, have often expressed their discomfort on including technology in natural settings – it somehow seems to be cheating. However, we studied whether engaging with nature through technology is likely to hinder the development of a relationship with the natural world. We asked two groups of volunteers to go out and notice three beautiful things in nature. Half of them had to simply note them in their heads. The other half had to take a digital picture with their mobile device. To our surprise,

---

16 M. Richardson and D. Sheffield, Three good things in nature: noticing nearby nature brings sustained increases in connection with nature, *PsyEcology* 8(1) (2017): 1-32.

both groups saw a significant rise in nature connection.[17] Especially when dealing with older children or adolescents, we have to meet them where they are – and, often, where they are is on their phones.

Another way to ensure children are engaging with the beauty found through the natural world is to set up art projects in, with and about nature. Consider the work of Andy Goldsworthy, for example, who uses natural materials and settings to enhance what is already there in nature (go on – google him now if you're not familiar with his work![18]), or another UK-based artist who works in and with nature, James Brunt.[19] Both work and play with the idea of ephemeral materials, enhancing and highlighting the landscape. Their art can inspire children to create similar site-specific sculptures or pictures, either alone or in teams. Consider leaving the art and materials where you found them, rather than bringing them indoors. Again, technology can be your friend – take pictures, or ask children to take pictures on your device and display in class later, but leave the art on site to be enjoyed, and changed by whatever natural or other processes occur.

Consider, of course, other types of artistic expression too – from poetry about nature, to capturing nature's beauty in drawings or paintings. Leaf printing, bark rubbing; there are many ways to incorporate nature into your art activities, and books and websites out there that will give you ideas on how to go about it. Ensure that when you do use

---

17 A. Barrable and D. Booth, Green and screen: does mobile photography enhance or hinder our connection to nature? *Digital Culture & Education* 12(2) (2020). Available at: https://static1.squarespace.com/static/5cf15af7a25999000170 6378/t/5f02e912b96a0625120affc5/1594026261822/Barrable+%26+Booth-merged.pdf.

18 See https://www.livingyourwildcreativity.com/art-gallery-1-mitchell-1.

19 See https://www.jamesbruntartist.co.uk.

natural materials in art, you treat nature with empathy and respect. Which brings us to …

NURTURING EMPATHY AND COMPASSION TOWARDS THE NATURAL WORLD

Before I go into this any further, I feel I need to define the terms used so we are all on the same page. Empathy is an ability, for most of us inherent, that allows us to feel the emotions of another (affective empathy) or to take the perspective of another being (cognitive empathy). Affective empathy starts very early; we can see it in babies when they participate in affective contagion – one baby cries and then the others join in! Cognitive empathy is developed a little later and is a little more complex, but most of us are quite skilful at empathy by the time we reach school age. Compassion, on the other hand, is a little more complex and it includes a desire to help. So, not only do we experience the feelings or perspective of another, but that stirs in us the beginnings of an action. Both of these are important in the development of a relationship, whether that is a relationship to other humans, or one with the natural world.

Many children will have a very developed sense of empathy already; for others, we need to verbalise, model and shape their experience in ways that enable them to access those important emotions and thoughts. An excellent way to do this is through caring for animals or plants. Growing plants from seed, whether indoors or outdoors, is a nurturing activity and one that tends to help children get in touch with their feelings of empathy towards the natural world. Gardening in schools is also linked to positive outcomes in relation to improving dietary choices and improved well-being.[20] And remember the Eurasian owl in my bathroom? Well, for me, watching my dad looking after injured animals was the start of a lifelong relationship with the natural world.

Even observing wild animals – talking about their needs, their rights and experience of the world – or looking after domesticated animals can also create this feeling of empathy. It doesn't have to be a dog or a cat (though there are some very fortunate schools that are able to bring such experiences to their learners); a fish tank or a snail farm (I had one for three years while teaching – it was a perfect classroom pet project) can be equally effective.

One of the mechanisms that research has found to be effective in bringing us closer and encouraging feelings of empathy with the natural world is anthropomorphism. Thinking about a tree as a friend, as described in the activity on page 61, or giving voice to a tree or plant in the grounds are excellent ways to bring this to life. Have a look in the Further Reading section for a link to a wonderful project that had citizens texting trees in their local area, as an example of how technology can enhance empathy towards nature and ultimately our experience of and relationship to the natural world.

MINDFULNESS

Despite the fact that mindfulness has become something of a buzzword in many contexts, including in education, and a panacea for a lot of the ills we suffer – from stress and burnout to attention deficit hyperactivity disorder

---

20 H. Ohly, S. Gentry, R. Wigglesworth, A. Bethel, R. Lovell and R. Garside, A systematic review of the health and well-being impacts of school gardening: synthesis of quantitative and qualitative evidence, *BMC Public Health* 16 (2016): 286.

(ADHD) – definitions of the term are contested. For this particular section, and keeping in mind that the mindfulness we are referring to is not therapeutic, but about something much simpler, I will keep two key components at the forefront: the first is about attention to the present moment or, as Bishop et al. state, 'the self-regulation of attention so that it is maintained on immediate experience, thereby allowing for increased recognition of mental events in the present moment';[21] the second component is that it should be characterised by curiosity, openness and acceptance. On the whole, you will notice that many young children often engage with nature in this way – focusing their attention on the moment, with curiosity and acceptance. Think of the toddler who follows a ladybird as it explores a leaf, or the wonder in the eyes of a child noticing icicles for the first time. However, in education we quite often pass by this wonder, openness and curiosity and focus on results, outcomes and activities. For once, when in nature, consider letting children indulge in being. The idea of being rather than doing can also be a helpful way to frame mindfulness. It is about the moment, and one of the easiest ways to fully be in the moment is by engaging our senses – bringing awareness to the moment. Introduce moments of silence where you just *are* – they don't have to be long – no doing, but simply being in the space with openness and curiosity. Ask children to engage with their senses. What can they smell? If they close their eyes, what can they hear? Mindfulness in this sense is not part of a formal practice – of meditation, for example, as some of us have experienced. It is more a way of engaging with our environment in the moment; of curiously exploring our experience and being attentive to our mind.

---

21 S. R. Bishop, M. Lau, S. Shapiro, L. Carlson, N. D. Anderson, J. Carmody et al., Mindfulness: a proposed operational definition, *Clinical Psychology: Science and Practice* 11(3) (2004): 230–241 at 230.

RESEARCH CASE STUDY: VISITING A NATURE RESERVE

Springfield Primary School is located fairly close to the centre of a medium-sized city but is also fortunate enough to be within a 15-minute walk of a small nature reserve. The Year 5 teachers have set up a regular slot where they walk to the reserve and undertake various activities with a focus on well-being and increasing social and nature connection. However, a lot of these activities are linked to the arts – music and drama, dance and visual arts. These are usually slotted into the medium-term plans at the beginning of each term, although there needs to be flexibility for when the weather does not allow for a certain activity to happen.

The two Year 5 classes visit every second Wednesday afternoon. After lunch they take the 15-minute walk – they have to take two other members of staff with them to comply with health and safety ratios. The children have risk assessed both the journey there and their time at the reserve. The teachers briefly go through the risk assessment each time, adjusting it to weather conditions or any incidents noted from previous times.

Once at the reserve, the children have a routine they repeat, that starts with *simply being*. They take a moment to use their senses to (re)connect with the place – how has it changed from last time? What is there that is new? They start by closing their eyes and mindfully listening for 2 minutes – focusing first on sounds far away, then on sounds closer by; not thinking about the sounds but experiencing them. They then open their eyes and look at their surroundings, mindfully engaging with nature near and far, noticing what's close by then looking far away. What often follows is a variety of games, some of which are linked to the expressive arts in the curriculum – the children will often make music or engage in drama games within the reserve. Other times they play a hunting game, where they pretend to be animals. One of the groups takes the role of hyenas and are the hunters, while the other group becomes the hunted antelopes. This is done in silence to, again, engage all the senses in the game and provide optimum immersion.

The school was part of a research study to look at how the visit and activities impact on the children's nature connection. When measuring nature connection before and after, we found that there were positive changes in most children who engaged in these activities. Moreover, we found positive changes in the children's mood.[22]

---

22 A. Barrable, D. Booth, D. Adams and G. Beauchamp, Enhancing nature connection and positive affect in children through mindful engagement with natural environments, *International Journal of Environmental Research and Public Health* 18(9) (2021): 4785.

TAKEAWAY POINTS

- The natural environment can be conducive to building positive relationships.

- There are many pedagogical aspects of nature-based learning that promote autonomy, competence and relatedness.

- Nature connection – our relationship to the natural world – is associated with increased well-being and pro-environmental behaviours.

- Contact alone is not enough to support nature connection; empathy, mindfulness and noticing beauty can be pathways towards a positive relationship with the natural world.

CHAPTER 4

ATTAINMENT

I can't start writing this section without first stating my reservations about distilling attainment into separate boxes, such as cognitive skills or curricular learning. Education is much more than that, and I imagine that if you are reading this book, you believe so too. However, research often works in boxes – and when looking at the evidence, it probably makes sense to focus on the constituent parts of the whole. Having said that, practice is exactly the opposite – it is holistic and defies pigeonholing. For that reason, I want you to read this chapter while keeping in mind what has come before, and consider all learning and being as a whole, rather than focusing on particular skills. Attainment is a factor of a myriad of variables as diverse as birthweight and nutrition, home environment and genetics, opportunities and aspirations. It cannot, and should not, be distilled down to simply cognitive or motor skills, though we do know that these too impact on overall attainment outcomes. This chapter is more about laying out the opportunities that nature-based learning can afford our children, and how the natural environment can improve learning and ultimately affect attainment.

IMPROVING COGNITIVE SKILLS

Cognitive skills are the basic skills of our brain that facilitate thinking, remembering, talking, learning and many other processes. They are usually split into various functions encompassing domains such as attention and memory, perception, learning and decision-making, and language processing. There is a host of research to suggest that being in natural landscapes has a positive effect on some of our cognitive skills – in particular, our attention. In fact, the effect on our attentional processes can be so big that nature walks have been recommended as a natural treatment to reduce hyperactivity and deficits in attention in children diagnosed with ADHD.[1] More on this in the next chapter.

We can see from the research that spending time in natural settings during early childhood seems to have a cumulative positive effect on a variety of cognitive outcomes. Evidence from a large study from Norway that followed more than 500 children for four years, suggests that the more time they spent outdoors in preschool, the better outcomes they had when in school.[2] The research team found a positive relationship between attention and memory, and time spent outdoors – and lower hyperactivity in the children who spent the most time in outdoor settings. To put it mildly, it seems that a wilder childhood, with more time spent playing and engaging with natural settings, prepares children well for the cognitive demands of school. This study is certainly not a one-off and not just limited to the early years; another even larger study from Spain that looked at children of school age (7–10 years old) and developmental trajectories of cognitive skills confirms this. The researchers measured working memory and inattentiveness at the beginning of the study, and 12 months later. Children who had more exposure to green areas, including through their school playground, surrounding

1   F. E. Kuo and A. Faber Taylor, A potential natural treatment for attention-deficit/ hyperactivity disorder: evidence from a national study, *American Journal of Public Health* 94(9) (2004): 1580-1586.

2   V. Ulset, F. Vitaro, M. Brendgen, M. Bekkhus and A. I. Borge, Time spent outdoors during preschool: links with children's cognitive and behavioral development, *Journal of Environmental Psychology* 52 (2017): 69-80.

school boundaries and other spaces, such as home and commuting route, showed better development of these skills.[3]

To put it simply, being in greener areas in our early and middle childhood allows for better development of cognitive skills such as attention and memory, which are crucial to academic success. As practitioners, especially if we are in the early years and primary, it makes sense to encourage children to spend as much time as possible outdoors, but also to work towards greening school playgrounds and gaining access to green spaces for all children.

NON-COGNITIVE SKILLS

Cognitive skills, such as those discussed above, are only part of the equation that contributes to academic attainment. Some of you may remember the famous Stanford marshmallow experiment (conducted by psychologist Walter Mischel).[4] If not, see if you can find a video of it – it is basically an exercise in impulse control. The idea is simple: a child is left in a room with a marshmallow in front of them. They are told that they can eat the marshmallow, but if they manage to wait until the researcher is back in the room, then they will be offered an additional marshmallow too. The study has been repeated several times, and has also been challenged, but follow-ups found that children who are able to delay gratification – that is, who

3   P. Dadvand, M. J. Nieuwenhuijsen, M. Esnaola, J. Forns, X. Basagaña, M. Alvarez-Pedrerol et al., Green spaces and cognitive development in primary schoolchildren, *Proceedings of the National Academy of Sciences* 112(26) (2015): 7937-7942.

4   W. Mischel, O. Ayduk, M. G. Berman, B. J. Casey, I. H. Gotlib, J. Jonides et al., 'Willpower' over the life span: decomposing self-regulation, *Social Cognitive and Affective Neuroscience* 6(2) (2011): 252-256.

are able to wait for the researcher to return to the room – have better academic outcomes, including in standardised tests.[5] (It is worth acknowledging that the original study was revisited two decades later, and although it did not fail to replicate the results, the effects found were much smaller, and sometimes not significant.[6])

It should come as no surprise to any parents or teachers that children who are able to control their impulses and have better overall self-discipline are more likely to do better in school. A lot of what we do in school, and a lot of what we expect children to do, relies on delaying gratification; undertaking an action now that will be good for our future self – sitting nicely to get golden time minutes, finishing your homework so you can play or, later on in our academic career, staying in to study for an exam instead of going out to party with our friends. It is interesting to see, then, that nature contact has been linked with increased self-discipline in a variety of contexts, including in children from Spain and the USA. Moreover, the benefits of nature on self-discipline seem to extend to all children, including children with ADHD and learning difficulties, and not just their neurotypical peers.[7]

Other non-cognitive skills, such as self-confidence, critical thinking and problem-solving, increased resilience and leadership skills, as well as improved communication, have also been reported as being associated with outdoor and

---

5   Y. Shoda, W. Mischel and P. K. Peake, Predicting adolescent cognitive and self-regulatory competencies from preschool delay of gratification: identifying diagnostic conditions, *Developmental Psychology* 26(6) (1990): 978.

6   T. W. Watts, G. J. Duncan and H. Quan, Revisiting the marshmallow test: a conceptual replication investigating links between early delay of gratification and later outcomes, *Psychological Science* 29(7) (2018): 1159-1177.

7   M. Kuo, M. Barnes and C. Jordan, Do experiences with nature promote learning? Converging evidence of a cause-and-effect relationship, *Frontiers in Psychology* 10 (2019): 305.

nature-based learning in general, although the strength of the evidence is not quite as robust.[8]

FINE MOTOR SKILLS

Nothing in the area of child development stands alone. Development of motor skills is an inseparable component of cognitive development and of the development of academic and non-academic skills.[9] And yet, it can often be overlooked – especially as we focus more closely on digital skills and as children are spending more time in adult-led indoor settings. In general, motor skills are split into two large categories: gross and fine. The former are skills that involve big movements, such as skipping, running, jumping and climbing, while the latter – fine motor skills – relate to the ability to make small and precise movements with our fingers, hands and wrists. Both gross and fine motor skills are crucial for the development of pre-literacy and literacy skills in early childhood and beyond.

In fact, when we look at the readiness of a child to undertake tasks such as writing, we can see a host of separate skills that need to be in place – not just involving the hands, but the whole body. (Please see Appendix 6 for a breakdown of fine motor skills that need to be in place for writing readiness, and how these can be promoted through loose-part nature play.) These skills can, of course,

---

8   S. Mirrahimi, N. M. Tawil, N. A. G. Abdullah, M. Surat and I. M. S. Usman, Developing conducive sustainable outdoor learning: the impact of natural environment on learning, social and emotional intelligence, *Procedia Engineering* 20 (2011): 389-396.

9   E. Escolano-Pérez, M. L. Herrero-Nivela and J. L. Losada (2020), Association between preschoolers' specific fine (but not gross) motor skills and later academic competencies: educational implications, *Frontiers in Psychology* 11: 1044.

be developed indoors but the open-ended natural loose parts – such as stones, sticks, pine cones, seeds, sand and mud – can be an excellent way to develop these skills. Moreover, because of the natural variation of these loose parts (the naturally occurring difference in their size and shape), children can actually choose what is right for their stage of development without losing confidence. So a 4-year-old may be able to pick small seeds or tiny stones and berries to decorate her mud pie, but a 2-year-old will choose bigger parts that fit his stage and abilities, without losing confidence or getting frustrated. The variety of textures found in nature can also help develop tactile awareness in young children.

GROSS MOTOR SKILLS

Studies from around the western world in the last few decades have brought attention to the fact that a lot of young children go into school (and beyond) lacking what have been called fundamental motor skills. These are split into locomotor skills (such as running, hopping, skipping and jumping), non-locomotor skills (such as bending, twisting and moving across different plains) and stability skills that rely on using balance. In general, naturescapes have been found to afford excellent opportunities to practise these key fundamental motor skills, especially locomotor and stability skills.[10]

---

10 C. Lim, A. M. Donovan, N. J. Harper, and P. J. Naylor, Nature elements and fundamental motor skill development opportunities at five elementary school districts in British Columbia, *International Journal of Environmental Research and Public Health* 14(10) (2017): 1279.

VESTIBULAR STIMULATION AND PROPRIOCEPTION

Contrary to what we learned in primary school (and what some of us taught in primary school too – myself included) we don't just have five senses. Quite important to our development is our sixth sense, or somatosensory system, which has several branches to it. It includes the way that we experience the world, and our position within it, through our bodies – for example, the way we feel pain and temperature, and our sense of movement and balance. This can be seen in the following diagram:

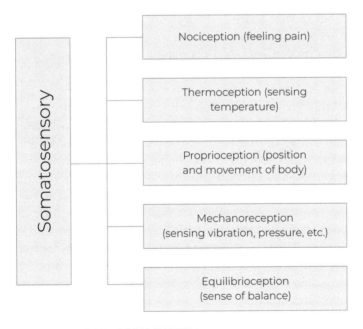

THE SOMATOSENSORY SYSTEM

In order for all these senses to be fully developed and integrated, it is essential that in infanthood and childhood we have adequate vestibular stimulation. In traditional societies this is easy to do – the young infant is carried on the back or front of the parent from very early on until they can safely walk around themselves. They are rocked and bounced naturally throughout the day as the main caregiver, usually the mother, carries them around. Not so in modern childhood. The baby is usually moved from the pushchair to the car seat to the high chair, with relatively few opportunities for the vestibular system, which is deep inside the inner ear, to be adequately stimulated.

A well-developed and typically responsive vestibular system gives a child feedback on where they are and enables them to feel secure and confident in their body. It allows the child to orient themselves in space, coordinate cross-body movements, and coordinate hands and eyes. It is, therefore, crucial for building pre-literacy skills, as well as fine and gross motor skills. In short, adequate vestibular stimulation can effectively improve postural control, support the development of fundamental motor skills and give a child confidence to move within their environment. Natural play spaces, where children can move within several planes of motion, are excellent for stimulating the vestibular system. Rocking, bouncing, rolling and swinging are all movements that happen quite naturally in outdoor environments, but are quite rare in indoor spaces. Ensuring that there are ropes for swinging, slopes for rolling and appropriate opportunities to move in different ways will support children's development in early childhood and beyond.

CASE STUDY: SUPPORTING PROPRIOCEPTION AND GROSS MOTOR SKILLS

Thomas is a 5-year-old whose gross motor skills are not as developed as those of other children of his age. He finds it hard to skip and jump with two legs, to go up and down stairs and to support himself when sitting. He is having weekly occupational therapy sessions, but is also participating in the school's nurture group, which includes a forest-school session once a week. Thomas loves forest school but finds that there are activities he is not able to do very well – like climbing trees, for example. The practitioners are aware of this, but also see where his strengths lie and how they can support him with building on the skills he already has. In consultation with Thomas's occupational therapist, the staff in the nurture group agree that the best way to support his development is to bring several large loose parts into the forest area. They set up ropes hanging from branches, but also on one of the slopes within the space. Thomas can then swing and pull himself up or lower himself down as needed. In this way he builds hand and upper-body strength. They bring in spare planks and pieces of tree trunk of various sizes and encourage the children to build bridges and practise balancing skills. Finally, they set up a swing that can provide Thomas with precious vestibular stimulation to support the development of all his other motor skills.

READY FOR LEARNING

As explained in detail in Chapter 1, where we looked at behaviour and our physiological responses to different environments, our optimal learning state is a quiet alertness – the state we find ourselves in when our parasympathetic response is activated. This rest and digest state, a state of relaxation, can only be achieved in contexts where we feel safe. Being in natural environments can help with this, so when considering spaces for learning, think about how nature can help bring about this optimal physiological state for learning.

It is also helpful to reflect upon the 'affective' effects of being in nature. It has reliably been shown that we are happier in nature; we experience improved mood. Coupled with the fact that engagement seems to be higher when we take children out of the classroom, it is no surprise that, on average, nature-based instruction has been found to be more effective than traditional instruction. Surprisingly, this holds for both teacher-led and curriculum activities, as well as child-led activities.[11] The research has been a little fuzzy for decades, especially because of the methods used to evaluate engagement – there was certainly a bias towards simply asking teachers and/or children to report on what they thought the outcomes were, or how much they enjoyed an activity. Of course, in this instance, participant and researcher bias could not be avoided, and in the case of children reporting, social desirability bias could also affect responses. However, newer research which has been using objective measures of performance, attainment and cognitive processes, has actually corroborated the increased effectiveness of nature-based instruction over traditional indoor teaching. To support this idea, we

---

11 Kuo et al., Do experiences with nature promote learning?

also see a dose–response relationship – meaning that the more natural the environment (in terms of plants and animals, time spent in nature or biodiversity measures), the bigger the benefit for the pupil.[12] As discussed earlier, this effect is not simply because of the setting, but it also relies on the pedagogical strategies that are often employed in outdoor settings, with more children having more autonomy and taking ownership of their own learning. In fact, the effect is likely to be determined by a variety of pathways, as are most robust phenomena in the social sciences, with a series of benefits to psychological, cognitive and physical states that ultimately promote better, more engaging and more effective learning.

THE IMPORTANCE OF AFFORDANCE (AND HOW YOU TOO CAN USE IT WHEN PLANNING)

There is, however, another aspect of natural environments, beyond their calming and attention-restoring properties, that should be of interest to educators: the concept of affordance. The idea of affordance is at once both very complex and extremely simple. It describes a fundamental principle that guides every organism's interaction with its surroundings and applies as much to ecology as it does to education, in my opinion. It is an idea that comes to us from ecology. First used in this way by psychologist James J. Gibson in the 1970s, it is a term devised to describe the relationship between an agent and a physical system or environment they find themselves in.

---

12 Kuo et al., Do experiences with nature promote learning?

The important point to remember is that each agent – in our instance, each different child – brings different strengths to the setting and, therefore, is able to yield different benefits from their interaction with it. Depending on their creativity, physical skills, prior knowledge and aptitudes, open-ended resources – such as those found in nature-based settings – become a blank cheque for the child. Learning in natural environments is akin to learning in a complex adaptive system, where current interactions influence future interactions, system-wide patterns emerge and there is constant feedback across all sections. Using this interactionist model of education and bringing in a third dynamic element (that of the curriculum) creates infinite possibilities.

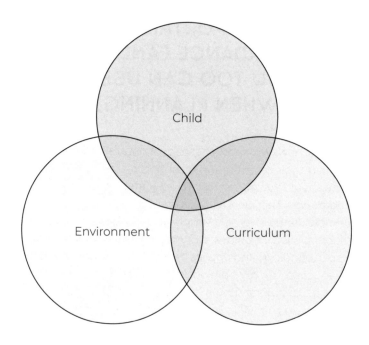

THE INTERSECTION OF CHILD, ENVIRONMENT AND CURRICULUM

Ideally, when planning for learning in natural environments you should take affordance into serious consideration. Part of your role in this scenario is not so much to guide learning, but to facilitate children's perception of affordances in nature for individualised benefits.[13] This requires a certain flexibility, good knowledge of the curriculum and even better communication with the children you are teaching. It also requires allowing for autonomy in the way children approach a topic. In the next two sections we will see how affordance, and planning for it flexibly, can support curricular learning.

SUPPORTING CURRICULAR LEARNING

Learning in natural environments, mostly outdoors, has been used for years to make significant contributions to curricular subjects. Below you can find some guidance on specific subjects and ways to bring nature alive in the learning, as well as the learning alive in nature.

LANGUAGE AND LITERACY

The biggest advantage you have when teaching language and literacy outdoors is the diverse vocabulary that is available to you. Nature can provide incredibly rich opportunities for spoken and written language. Taking advantage of nature as a starting point, you can consider building a lesson *around* and *about* nature that is not necessarily *in* nature. The outdoor part of your lesson does not have to be long; a lesson can start with a provocation outdoors, with careful exploration and observation, and then take

---

13 V. Sharma-Brymer, E. Brymer, T. Gray and K. Davids, Affordances guiding forest school practice: the application of the ecological dynamics approach, *Journal of Outdoor and Environmental Education* 21 (2018): 103-115.

place indoors where children use the inspiration they have gained outdoors as a starting point. Story crafting, poetry writing and descriptive nature writing can all happen in this way.

For younger children who are still in the early levels of literacy, the outdoors can be a very rich environment to support mark-making, initial sound-hunting and to support phonics development. For older children, when the weather is good, consider bringing reading outdoors – either reading aloud or individual quiet reading.

MATHS OUTDOORS

As Juliet Robertson writes in the excellent *Messy Maths*, 'the world is a mathematical place'.[14] It does take a creative and committed educator to map out all areas of mathematics to outdoors provision, but it should be easier with Juliet's guidance. All learning, but particularly mathematics, is a very social and collaborative experience for young children – and this is something you should consider when planning for maths in nature. To do so, you need to take into account the affordance of your space, and consider the interactions of the child with the landscape and the opportunities for learning that are hidden in the nature outside your door. The use of mathematical language, the spotting and sharing of patterns and the questioning of mathematical concepts should underlie most of your maths in nature provision. Physically, the use of loose parts (yes, sticks!) and embodied learning that can take place can guide your practice.

---

14 J. Robertson, *Messy Maths: A Playful, Outdoor Approach for Early Years* (Carmarthen: Independent Thinking Press, 2017), p. 1.

SCIENCE

Teaching science outdoors, as well as technology and engineering, is nothing new – in fact, most early science was about the natural world and relied on careful observation and exploration of changes within it. When in nature, even in free play, most children will end up involved in scientific exploration, whether it be pushing someone on a swing or observing a bee gathering pollen from a flower. For more structured approaches, and when planning delivery of curricular topics, go back to the affordances of the place and consider the natural elements you have to work with. Pedagogically speaking, enquiry- and project-based learning are best suited for teaching science, technology, engineering and mathematics (STEM) outdoors, rather than a more prescriptive direct instruction approach. This is not to say that direct instruction does not have its place in education – it does and it is certainly valuable – it's just that its place is not in the outdoors; keep it for inside, before or after the child-led enquiry learning has taken place.

CASE STUDY: BEACH SCHOOL FOR STEM

Winter on the east coast of Scotland is not the mildest, and this day is no exception. Just as well that the children are dressed appropriately for the final session of their topic on polar explorers. The topic has included a trip to the Royal Research Ship *Discovery* in Dundee and plenty of opportunities for STEM learning, including engineering challenges, climate change and food chains.[15] Today's session, however, is very different and will take place at the beach. The challenge is rather simple: each team has a wooden box full of supplies that they need to carry from one side of the beach to the other. They have ropes and various other materials that may be used. The discussion starts in the classroom and each team gets a chance to make hypotheses about what may work well. The main outcome for this lesson is related to learning about forces and investigating friction (by investigating how friction affects motion, children can suggest ways to improve efficiency in moving objects). The time in the classroom certainly gives Mr Barnett a good idea of the pupils' current understanding, but the magic happens when they head outdoors! The practical element of dragging their supplies across the beach on this bright but very chilly day brings learning to life! The 10-year-old polar explorers have to call upon previous knowledge, work together in teams, make the most of each trial and learn from each error. After the hour is over, they have successfully brought their supplies across the beach, and have, with the help of Mr Barnett, lit a fire and sit around it for a chat. They will write about their experience tomorrow – 'The Diary of a Polar Explorer' – for now they will enjoy their steaming cups of hot chocolate.

---

15 See https://www.stem.org.uk/sites/default/files/pages/downloads/Polar%20 Explorer%20activity%20pack.pdf.

ADDING INFORMATION TECHNOLOGY

I am often met with enquiring glances and questioning faces when I mention that nature-based learning is ideal for working with certain types of technology. But hear me out! The 'green versus screen' dichotomy often heard in the press, or discussions about how our children spend their time, is a false one – and also very ableist; in the case of children with additional needs, technology can provide a way to meaningfully engage with nature (see Chapter 5). Sometimes screen time can facilitate green time and can break down barriers in engaging with nature on our children's own terms and following their interests. So, moving away from the either/or model, how can technology enhance or facilitate nature contact and nature-based education?

Going back to the start and looking at the aims of nature-based education, we find many that intersect with those of technology education: enhancing engagement, improving social skills and communication, accessing new learning and supporting well-being and nature connection. None of these are inherently incompatible with the use of technology, and many of them can actually be enhanced by the use of relevant technological features such as mobile phones, cameras, GPS devices, etc.

Essentially, in order to integrate technology into your session, it has to start with planning. The main questions are:

● What are my aims for this nature-based session?

● Can technology act in a complementary way?

If the answer to the second question is yes, then ask yourself how best to integrate technology into your sessions (see Further Reading for some apps that may be of use to you). There are also caveats, as there are certainly times where it is not appropriate to use technology – for example, in extreme weather, during free play and when there are hazards that need 100% attention on the task at hand (this should be part of your risk assessment in the first place).

Activities can vary but, in general, consider using cameras or other recording devices to enhance and entice children into observation. Taking photos, making a video or a recording, and manipulating images or sounds can all be ways to focus attention more keenly. In research that was undertaken, participants with a camera were found to have 'better recognition of aspects of the scene that they photographed than of aspects they did not photograph. Furthermore, participants who used a camera during their experience recognised even non-photographed aspects better than participants without a camera did'.[16] In this way, you can also use images taken by the children at a later date for a variety of purposes, including writing or art prompts. Cameras, both static and video, can also be used to record change and compare before and after, or create a time lapse. This is particularly useful if you are looking at processes in science and provides an excellent way of recording and assessing. Finally, the use of specific apps can give access to rather specialised knowledge, let children take part in citizen science projects and even pro-mote nature connection (see Further Reading).

---

16 A. Barasch, K. Diehl, J. Silverman and G. Zauberman, Photographic memory: the effects of volitional photo taking on memory for visual and auditory aspects of an experience, *Psychological Science* 28(8) (2017): 1056–1066 at 1065.

ACTIVITY: GREEN AND SCREEN

This is a simple activity that can be done with any age – I have used it with children as young as 4 and young adults at university level with success. The power of this exercise is in its simplicity, and you can, of course, include additional activities before or after.

The aim is to capture some of the beauty of nature around the school grounds. Depending on the age of the children, you can use school devices in groups, or let secondary pupils use their own electronic devices. They should look for three beautiful images of the natural world (although there are variations where you may want to capture sounds as well). These are then to be shared, talked about, printed and displayed, used for additional activities (like drawing or writing poetry), tweaked or enhanced using filters or other technology. Nothing is off-limits – the pupils' point of view about what is beautiful in nature can be celebrated and shared. If done regularly, say once a term, you can compare images from different seasons and mark the passing of time. You may also want to create a competition for the most creative/beautiful/colourful/impactful image. The activity, while simple, offers many extension opportunities (and research suggests that it can increase connection to nature[17]).

The takeaway is short: don't hesitate to use technology to engage, enhance and entice! Plan it into your experience, working back from your aims. Be prepared: as any teacher knows, technology can often go wrong – have a plan B (and C). And, finally, go out and have fun!

---

17 Barrable and Booth, Green and screen.

DIFFERENTIATION

Differentiation, which is the tailoring of the learning, instruction, process or learning context to suit particular children's needs, is one of the most high-impact strategies in education, and yet one of the most challenging to achieve. The focus on equity, rather than equality, of giving each child what they need to grow and succeed, and meeting them where they are, can ensure that all children feel valued and competent within your class (for more on how competence fosters well-being and good behaviour, see Chapter 3). As a general rule, successful differentiation will increase individual pupil attainment, engagement and motivation.

There are three basic ways of delivering differentiated instruction (although there are also many subtler ways and combinations that can be used by the experienced teacher); two of the most common methods are to differentiate by adjusting either the content or the outcome. However, when we talk about nature-based learning, a key advantage is that we can often differentiate by adjusting the process too. Let's break it down.

Adjusting content is common but particularly hard to do, especially in big classes or when you have several levels that children are working at. It basically relies on delivery of different content according to each child's or group's ability, while the mode of instruction usually stays the same. Quite often, this type of differentiation means that the teacher focuses on lower-ability pupils or groups, while the more able are left to their own devices.

When a teacher chooses to adjust the outcome of a lesson, they are tailoring the success criteria or desirable end outcome of the lesson for each group or pupil. This is particularly useful in open-ended tasks and learning, and can be used in nature settings easily, as pupils can choose their resources and shape their own outcomes. Going back to the aforementioned affordances (see page 81), planning around your space, its affordance and capacity for interaction with your learners is key here.

Finally, when you consider differentiation through process, nature pedagogy offers plenty to work with. Project-based learning is particularly attractive in natural contexts, and very suited to this kind of differentiation. Given the likelihood of nature-based learning happening in bigger spaces, grouping, for example, is an effective way to differentiate by process; same- or mixed-ability groupings (depending on the desired outcome) and freedom to choose different approaches as a group offers flexibility.

As part of the greater autonomy that nature pedagogy affords, and sometimes demands, tasks designed to develop metacognition skills and taking responsibility for their own learning can also be very effective. Reflecting on past gains, setting own goals (differentiated, as each child reflects on their own experience, and sets their own goals moving forward) can also be used. Finally, and again linked to greater autonomy, consider voice and choice in process and outcome. For more information on valuing and including children's voice in your teaching, see Chapter 5.

TAKEAWAY POINTS

- Research has shown that being around natural environments in childhood has a positive effect on cognitive development.

- Nature's physiological effects on us create an ideal learning environment.

- The affordances of natural spaces offer endless possibilities for rich teacher-led and pupil-led learning.

- Technology can be employed in complementary ways to support nature-based learning.

CHAPTER 5

INCLUSION

I have been challenging myself to see inclusion more broadly than simply catering to children with disabilities within our mainstream setting, but instead as a response that acknowledges and supports the diversity among our pupil body. It is about recognising that we are all different, with diverse needs, challenges and strengths. This good practice needs to extend beyond the classroom and into all our educational activities, including nature-based learning. In this chapter we will look at some of the benefits and opportunities that natural learning environments can offer children with additional needs – in fact, in certain instances, nature-based learning can offer additional benefits to children who are neurodivergent – but also consider some of the challenges we need to reflect upon to ensure equitable access for all. The two basic premises of inclusive education remain: we want our provision to be constantly developing – and therefore, by recognising that one size does not fit all, we accept that our practice needs to be responsive to the developing need of all our learners; and secondly, we need an iterative process of identifying and removing barriers.[1]

It is hard to write a chapter that will encompass the vast diversity of needs and of shaping provision for our pupils who have additional needs. For this reason, and in the first instance, I want to give you the tools to use pupil voice and co-creation to shape the environment in ways that are accessible to those with different needs, in accordance with the two basic premises mentioned above. The princi-

---

1   M. Ainscow, T. Booth, A. Dyson, P. Farrell, J. Frankham, F. Gallannaugh et al., *Improving Schools, Developing Inclusion* (London: Routledge, 2006).

ples and tools presented here can be used with all children to ensure they have a say in the shaping of their own provision, but can be specifically targeted to children with additional needs, in an effort to acknowledge and tackle barriers to access that we may not have considered.

PUPIL VOICE

What are the possibilities when we stop doing and we listen to the children we teach? What happens when our pupils have a say in matters that pertain to their own lives? Research suggests that listening to pupil voice enhances engagement with learning and well-being.[2] Truly listening to our pupils gives them the message that we care, that they are important to us and that they have control over their lives. However, as Laura Lundy, professor of international children's rights at Queen's University, Belfast, characteristically writes, 'voice is not enough'.[3] Following her model, and considering the rights of children, as embodied by the United Nations Convention on the Rights of the Child, and more specifically Article 12 – the right of the child to participation – provision needs to be broader.

On top of that, by considering ways to bring forth and to listen to children's views on matters that affect them, we need to go beyond the tokenistic. If planning to facilitate such a process, there are four separate yet interrelated and somewhat chronological aspects: space, voice, audience and influence. In very simple terms, we need to provide a

2 R. J. Alexander, C. Doddington, J. Gray, L. Hargreaves and R. Kershner (eds.), *The Cambridge Primary Review Research Surveys* (London: Routledge, 2010).

3 L. Lundy, 'Voice' is not enough: conceptualising Article 12 of the United Nations Convention on the Rights of the Child, *British Educational Research Journal* 33(6) (2007): 927–942.

safe space and opportunities for children to express their views, and facilitate that expression as best we can. Once this is done, it is paramount that the views expressed must be listened to, taken into account and have some impact.[4] The following case study can give you an idea of how this can be enacted.

RESEARCH CASE STUDY: CHILDREN'S VOICE TO SHAPE SPACE IN AN EARLY CHILDHOOD SETTING

The new nursery building is beautiful; big windows, airy spaces, the indoors has been shaped with the needs of children in mind. The outdoors, however, not so much. The ample-sized playground has been designed to look more like the car park of a posh hotel than a space to be used and enjoyed by young children. Much of it is paved and the grass has been blocked off by rows of bushes, so children have difficulty accessing it – and the few mature trees that were within the grounds have no access to them as they are surrounded by fencing.

The staff can see the possibilities of shaping the space but aren't sure where to start. That's where we come in. Led by Dr Boath, we are brought in to work with the children as potential enablers, to guide and assist them, not only in the expression, but also in the formation of their views. The first step was to invite children aged 2–4 to look at different potential spaces they

---

4   See https://ec.europa.eu/info/sites/default/files/lundy_model_of_
    participation.pdf.

might like. This is important as children need all the information available to make informed decisions. For this, a few children were chosen by their peers to travel to nearby nurseries with developed spaces, to take pictures. We also took pictures of other settings that the children could not visit. The images, which were printed out, were then offered out to the children to have a look at. Before we began we explained that there was no pressure to participate, yet all were invited to do so. For this reason, we set up a table with a variety of materials for the children to express their views. Some just looked at the pictures and talked to us about them, some decided to draw what their favourite place would look like.

Children had a lot to say about what they liked doing outdoors, and how they wanted to engage with the space. True to affordance theory, discussed in length in Chapter 4, they saw the space as an invitation to inter-act, so they talked of features as facilitating different type of play or engagement. A box was seen as an opportunity to jump, pots and pans as a chance to play music. Fire was an incredibly attractive feature, much to the alarm of many of the staff. By shaping the space in ways the children had chosen, the practitioners put the children's needs and interests first, gave them the message that they matter and that their views were important in matters that affect them. Finally, a truly engaging and relevant space was designed to enable the children to play outdoors.[5]

---

5   L. Boath and A. Barrable, The child as co-researcher in the early years: what do children like in the outdoors?, *SERA Researching Education Bulletin* 9 (2020): 34-38.

In the case of children with additional needs, and depending on what those are, it may seem harder to involve them in the process, and due steps need to be taken to facilitate full access. As with all children, it is their right to be involved in decision-making in matters that pertain to them, and they should be provided with disability and age-appropriate assistance to realise that right. Including parents, carers or people who know the child and their needs well can help us to access their views. It is also a case of finding the right tools to help everyone communicate – so consider using different vehicles, including audio and video, drawings and writings, as well as augmentative and alternative communication.

Aside from shaping the environment and providing equal access to nature for all our pupils, it is important to acknowledge that nature can sometimes act therapeutically or preventatively for a lot of children with additional needs. For others, especially those with sensory processing difficulties, natural environments may be overwhelming. In the following sections I will try and cover some of the major opportunities and challenges that arise in nature-based learning for neurodivergent children.

ACTIVITY: MY PERFECT DAY IN NATURE

This is an indoor activity focused on eliciting children's ideas that can be incorporated into future outdoor activities. Depending on the ages of your pupils, or even on their preferences, choose the medium or media through which they will present their perfect day in nature; it could be a drawing or a collage, a poem, some writing or even a comic strip.

Before starting, brainstorm ideas about what people do in natural spaces; some will certainly have experiences from home but others might not, so ensure that, by the time they begin the activity, they have an informed opinion and an idea of the possibilities. Nature can be anywhere so, again, share with children the type of spaces they may travel to in their imaginations – it could be a local urban park, a remote spot in the countryside, the seaside; or they can even decide to go further afield – a tropical island, the Amazon rainforest or the Arctic. What does it feel like to be there? What can they see, hear, feel or taste?

Going from the imaginary immersive experience to the end product can be individual – each child works on their own. If you have time and wish to, let the children share. From these activities, note down at least one point from each child's description that can be used for future reference: for example, Amir is keen to look for bugs while Anna wants to spend time alone in nature; Lloyd wants to climb trees while Sam prefers to draw birds. Some will need to be adapted – not much chance of tracking polar bears in the Arctic, but perhaps you can watch a documentary. Keep a wish list of these activities and see how many you can complete before the end of the school year. Alternatively, put them in a hat/jar and draw one each week. This activity highlights the value of each child's wish, puts them in the driving seat in terms of how they want to engage, but also keeps a playful, adventurous and inclusive spirit in nature engagement.

NEURODIVERGENT CHILDREN

ADHD

As a teacher, it is very likely that you will have some experience of teaching children with ADHD – it is, after all, the most common neurobehavioural disorder in childhood, with an estimated 3–5% of children affected.[6] It is more common in boys and is characterised by persistent and unusually high levels of inattention, impulsivity and/or hyperactivity. These can interfere with social and academic aspects of life for the child and can be difficult to manage. Wouldn't it be great if there was a safe and natural treatment? It turns out that there may just be. Several studies have indicated that green or natural settings can have a positive impact on ADHD symptoms across diverse populations of children.

As we saw in earlier chapters, in the general population, and across both children and adults, our attention is enhanced and restored when we are in the presence of natural environments, and after our exposure to them. Studies that have looked at children with ADHD further support this effect; for example, a study that looked at concentration and attention levels of children with ADHD before and after a walk in the park, found that walking in green nature had a positive effect.[7] In fact, even when compared to medication such as methylphenidate, also

---

6   NHS England, *Delivering Effective Services for Children and Young People with ADHD: Good Practice Guidance for Commissioners and Service Providers across Greater Manchester* (2018), p. 8. Available at: https://www.england.nhs.uk/north-west/wp-content/uploads/sites/48/2019/03/GM-wide-ADHD-guidance.pdf.

7   Kuo and Faber Taylor, A potential natural treatment for attention-deficit/hyperactivity disorder.

known as Ritalin, the effect of a dose of nature was similar, without any of the side effects.

Supporting children with ADHD in mainstream settings can pose many challenges, but consider how a 20-minute break in a natural setting can benefit subsequent tasks and make time in the classroom much more effective. Given that all children benefit from such breaks that restore attention, consider fitting in 'micro breaks' during the day, between lessons or to break up longer sessions and restore attention for all.

It is not just that nature can be *therapeutic* in this scenario, but it is also likely that there is a *protective* effect of nature. As discussed in earlier chapters, when we look at the cognitive skills that develop in early childhood and how spending time in natural environments can actually boost and support optimal development, there seems to be a protective effect of nature on the development of ADHD. In a large New Zealand cohort study (meaning a study that followed thousands of children from birth through adolescence and into adulthood), environmental epidemiologists found that living in a rural location in early childhood, or having increased access to green landscapes, meant that a child had a reduced risk of developing ADHD.[8]

This supports previous research from Norway which showed improved attention and reduced hyperactivity in school-aged children who had spent more time outdoors during preschool.[9] Although this should have implications at a policy and national planning level, we can, as practitioners, be a positive influence for the children in our care.

---

8   G. Donovan, Y. Michael, D. Gatziolis, A. 't Mannetje and J. Douwes, Exposure to the natural environment and rurality is protective of ADHD in a large birth cohort of New Zealand children, *Environmental Epidemiology* 3 (2019): 103.

9   Ulset et al., Time spent outdoors during preschool.

Regular and sustained access to natural spaces for play, exercise and rest should be built into the daily routine of young children to support optimal development.

Before I move on, it is important to take note of a common challenge that may arise in relation to children with ADHD when playing freely in natural environments: in general, people of all ages with ADHD tend to engage more readily in risky behaviours, and can sometimes put themselves at higher risk of physical injury.[10] The reasons are multiple and complex, but most likely stem from a combination of impaired risk perception (they may not be able to judge relative risk as well as others) and a lack of inhibition behaviours (they might not be able to halt an impulse to behave in a certain way). For practitioners working with children with ADHD in a risky play situation, it is even more important to undertake the joint risk assessment, as proposed in Chapter 2. This should be done together and regularly, both as a reminder to the child, and as an active practice of the skill of risk assessment, which the child will get better at the more they practise.

AUTISM SPECTRUM

Autism can impact on a person's perception and socialisation, social interaction and communication. Given that it is a spectrum, we need to remember that the abilities and needs of each autistic individual vary greatly, as do the expected outcomes. Discussing autism in nature-based education with practitioners, researchers and people with lived experience, one aspect resonated most strongly with me: the framing of expectations when we look at outcomes. Framing matters, as does the language we use to

---

10 T. W. Boyer, The development of risk-taking: a multi-perspective review, *Developmental Review* 26(3) (2006): 291–345.

talk about challenges and opportunities. Older practice and research often uses a deficit-based framing, where the desired outcome is a reduction in autistic symptomatology. I can't help but agree with University of Cambridge researcher Samantha Friedman, who specialises in autism and nature, when she told me, 'I think nature should be used to support autistic kids in being their most genuine, mentally healthy selves, not reducing parts of them that aren't socially normative!' With this in mind, let's see how we can do just that: supporting the autistic children in our care in becoming and being their most genuine, mentally healthy selves.

As with all that we do with our learners, and especially when considering shaping our provision to meet individual needs, eliciting and enabling pupil voice and ensuring it has impact has to be at the heart of our practice. This may be more complicated in the case of children who are non-speaking or who have more complex needs, but the process remains the same in that they need to be present in discussions about them and their future and offered appropriate opportunities to contribute. Consider inviting parents/guardians or even siblings who know them well and may be able to help articulate their strengths and challenges.

There is some literature out there that has looked at the development of autism on a population level, and has found that more green space, especially tree cover, is associated with lower autism prevalence in children – this seems particularly true in areas with high road density.[11] This could be to do with air pollution levels, or may be altogether an incidental finding, with more research needed. Another study has found that tree-canopy coverage seems

11   J. Wu and L. Jackson, Inverse relationship between urban green space and childhood autism in California elementary school districts, *Environment International* 107 (2017): 140-146.

to predict fewer behaviour problems in autistic children, such as behaving in aggressive or socially inappropriate ways and ignoring requests,[12] although more research is required to look at whether the effect stands, and what the mechanism may be.

Research more specific on how nature can help autistic individuals flourish is still in its early stages, led by researchers such as Samantha Friedman, as well as by many autistic individuals and practitioners. Some of the smaller exploratory studies and reports from the ground support the intuitive idea that nature really can be transformative for autistic individuals, as it is for the rest of us. Reading through some of the literature, I am deeply moved by the words of the autistic teenager from the book *The Reason I Jump* – a powerful account of an autistic child's life: 'Just by looking at nature, I feel as if I'm being swallowed up into it ... Nature calms me down when I'm furious and laughs with me when I'm happy.'[13]

In the case of working with autistic individuals, as with most children who may have different social and sensory needs, I would like to propose moving forward with a dual model of seizing the opportunities and acknowledging (and mitigating for) the challenges. I will try to outline some examples below but would urge you to co-design this with the children, and their carer/parent when appropriate, giving them voice, helping them articulate their strengths and acknowledging that you can work with them on their challenges, in partnership. This is a similar process to using an individual education plan and could,

12 B. Barger, L. R. Larson, S. Ogletree, J. Torquati, S. Rosenberg, C. J. Gaither et al., Tree canopy coverage predicts lower conduct problem severity in children with ASD, *Journal of Mental Health Research in Intellectual Disabilities* 13 (2020): 43-61.

13 N. Higashida, *The Reason I Jump*, tr. K. A. Yoshida and D. Mitchell (New York: Penguin Random House, 2007), p. 119.

in fact, be incorporated into the same meeting and review schedule.

SEIZING THE OPPORTUNITIES

As with neurotypical children and adults, there are many benefits to engaging with nature-based education. Forest school in particular, with its emphasis on autonomy and the central role of the child as an agent, has been found to offer many opportunities that education inside the classroom doesn't. Making friends, trying new things and being challenged, and having new learning experiences have been identified as some of the benefits.[14] As with all children, having the opportunity to regularly experience success in challenging tasks can be a key desired outcome that boosts self-esteem and creates feelings of self-efficacy that can spill over into other activities. When talking to Samantha, who aside from being a researcher is also an experienced forest-school practitioner, she explains to me that a clear structure can increase accessibility as many autistic children thrive in predictable environments. Balancing structure and autonomy is therefore key in reaping all the benefits of the space. Setting up rituals and routines that are predictable can work wonders to the feelings of safety that a child experiences.

Another opportunity that nature affords autistic children is the option of stimming (Samantha has identified this in her research with autistic adults). Stimming – the making of stereotyped or repetitive movements and noises – can help some autistic children to manage their emotions, both positive and negative, and self-regulate when in situ-

---

14 K. Bradley and D. Male, 'Forest School is muddy and I like it': perspectives of young children with autism spectrum disorders, their parents and educational professionals, *Educational and Child Psychology* 34(2) (2017): 80–96.

ations that may otherwise be overwhelming. It is important that stimming is explained to both adults and children within the group, and accepted as a perfectly healthy tool for autistic (and non-autistic) people. In a study that asked autistic adults on their views on stimming, the authors report that: 'Autistic adults highlighted the importance of stimming as an adaptive mechanism that helps them to soothe or communicate intense emotions or thoughts and thus objected to treatment that aims to eliminate the behaviour.'[15] This is key for practitioners seeking to provide a supportive experience for all children in their setting.

ACKNOWLEDGING THE CHALLENGES

While some autistic people find nature soothing and an opportunity to engage in activities associated with their interests and on their own terms, there is research to suggest that for others, nature can be stressful. A US study explored both neurotypical and autistic children's anxiety levels in relation to exposure to green spaces and treescapes. The researchers found that autistic children may not experience the stress-busting benefits of being exposed to nature that we see in neurotypical children, as was presented earlier.[16] This could be because many autistic children experience sensory differences, meaning that some of their senses may be over- or under-sensitive.

15 S. K. Kapp, R. Steward, L. Crane, D. Elliott, C. Elphick, E. Pellicano et al., 'People should be allowed to do what they like': autistic adults' views and experiences of stimming, *Autism* 23(7) (2019): 1782-1792.

16 L. R. Larson, B. Barger, S. Ogletree, J. Torquati, S. Rosenberg, C. J. Gaither et al., Gray space and green space proximity associated with higher anxiety in youth with autism, *Health & Place* 53 (2018): 94-102.

These differences can and often do influence their feelings and actions – for example, a child who experiences sensory overload may react in a variety of ways: with withdrawal or with distressed behaviours. This is because too much sensory information can cause stress or anxiety, or even physical pain for the autistic person, who may then respond by shutting down, withdrawing or having a meltdown. It is important to recognise that natural environments can actually be very stimulating to the senses and can cause a sensory overload – this may be the case for some autistic children, while others may find being in nature soothing. In fact, many autistic people find nature sounds a lot more tolerable than man-made ones. The effect may even vary not just from individual to individual, but also from day to day, depending on weather conditions or other variables.

Engaging with nature can look very different for each autistic child and in each moment, Samantha Friedman reminds me. Some will seek out sensory input, while others won't: 'A child sitting alone in the grass who appears to be staring into space may be attuned to exactly what they need in that moment. Another child who is digging in squishy mud and talking to friends could be addressing the sensory needs they have. Both are doing exactly what's right for them, but one will appear to be more engaged with nature.'[17] Problem-solve with the child to increase accessibility, finding solutions to the challenges and making the experience a positive one. Reducing sensory overwhelm in ways like these can give the child opportunities to engage in sensory exploration that can be extremely beneficial. Other options include the use of sunglasses, for children who find the light or dappled shadow overwhelming, long sleeves or a light jacket to dampen the effect of the wind, and staying away from

17 Personal correspondence.

sand for those who find the texture uncomfortable or triggering. Samantha tells me of a child who used technology to help him deal with sensory overload, listening to music through headphones when entering a natural space to drown out the excited shouts and shrieks of other children, which he found overwhelming.

My own son, who attended a nature nursery, found the dappled sunshine particularly bothersome on sunny days – providing sunglasses to wear as needed soon fixed the issue and he was able to access all the benefits the setting could offer him. It is important to acknowledge that there is sometimes discomfort in nature and ensure that the individual feels safe and supported in their experience. A way to do this is to offer autonomy and very clear choice. When talking with practitioners who work with autistic and other neurodivergent children, they made it clear that consent is sought each and every time there is a forest-school session.

We all feel 'off' on occasion and when an autistic person does so, they may find certain situations overwhelming. It is important to have the choice to *not* join in if that is the case, where alternative plans should be made. It should be celebrated that the individual is able to be aware of their needs and communicate them clearly – a very positive step towards self-regulation and communication!

ADVERSE CHILDHOOD EXPERIENCES AND TRAUMA

In the last decade there has been a lot of talk and some increasing awareness of the prevalence of adverse childhood experiences (ACEs) within the general population, and their effects. For teachers, it is important to know that regardless of the area in which you teach, or its socio-economic level, you will come across children who have experienced adversity. It is astonishing to consider that 50% of the general population will have experienced at least one adverse or traumatic event in childhood, while up to one in five will have experienced three or more.[18] These experiences include domestic violence, neglect, parental separation and living with a parent with a mental health condition. Other experiences have also been flagged up, such as poverty – especially when it is long term.[19]

The bad news is that experiencing such adversity can have an effect on both our physical and mental health – both in the short and longer term. Research suggests that people with ACEs are more likely to go to prison and commit violence, develop heart disease and/or diabetes, and take part in health-harming behaviours, such as overeating or alcohol/drug abuse.[20] The way this happens is multi-factorial, as are most complex phenomena, and has its roots in our neurophysiology and the way in which stress, especially prolonged stress, affects our brain and the rest of our body. A chemical cascade of cortisol and adrenaline can become detrimental – especially to the young and developing brain – particularly when it is sustained over time. There is then a domino effect, with impacts on social relationships, psychological health and physical health.

The good news is that such experiences don't *have to* be detrimental – and that there are protective and therapeu-

---

18 M. T. Merrick, D. C. Ford, K. A. Ports and A. S. Guinn, Prevalence of adverse childhood experiences from the 2011-2014 behavioral risk factor surveillance system in 23 states, *JAMA Pediatrics* 172(11) (2018): 1038-1044.

19 M. Hughes and W. Tucker, Poverty as an adverse childhood experience, *North Carolina Medical Journal* 79(2) (2018): 124-126.

20 See http://www.healthscotland.scot/population-groups/children/adverse-childhood-experiences-aces/overview-of-aces.

tic factors. We know from studies looking at children who have experienced ACEs but have not gone on to develop the challenges mentioned above, that community resilience and strong family relationships can be protective;[21] think of them as a defence against that aforementioned domino effect. More recent research has identified nature and regular access to natural environments as another factor that may be protective and therapeutic.[22]

The physiological and psychological benefits of being in nature, as described in Chapter 2, can ameliorate some of the impact of ACEs on young people. Natural environments can act as a buffer for some of the toxic stress that is experienced during ACEs.[23] This can be seen at a purely physiological level, for example, when looking at levels of cortisol – a stress hormone that, with chronic exposure, can have a host of detrimental effects to health and well-being. We now know that people who are exposed to nature regularly have lower cortisol levels.[24] At the same time, the psychological effects of being in nature – such as greater autonomy, increased feelings of well-being and a sense of belonging that can often be part of nature-based education experiences – can act both protectively and

---

21 Adverse Childhood Experience (ACE) Support Hub Cymru, *What Works to Prevent Adverse Childhood Experiences (ACEs) at the Community Level?* (2021). Available at: https://phwwhocc.co.uk/wp-content/uploads/2022/02/What-Works-to-Prevent-ACEs-at-the-Community-Level.-An-Evidence-Review-Mapping-Exercise-Executive-Summary.pdf

22 A. K. Touloumakos and A. Barrable, Adverse childhood experiences: the protective and therapeutic potential of nature, *Frontiers in Psychology* 11 (2020): 597935.

23 C. Ward Thompson, P. Aspinall, J. Roe, L. Robertson and D. Miller, Mitigating stress and supporting health in deprived urban communities: the importance of green space and the social environment, *International Journal of Environmental Research and Public Health* 13 (2016): 440.

24 M. R. Hunter, B. W. Gillespie and S. Y. P. Chen, Urban nature experiences reduce stress in the context of daily life based on salivary biomarkers, *Frontiers in Psychology* 10 (2019): 722.

therapeutically for children who are currently experiencing adversity.

For you, as the practitioner, this may mean you try and offer more regular access to nature and green spaces, and try to take learning outdoors when you can. When working therapeutically with these children in the context of a nurture group, for example, or one-to-one, consider the importance of the natural environment and the potential for it to act as an extra layer or element of support in building resilience.

TAKEAWAY POINTS

- Nature can have a therapeutic effect on children with additional needs (for example, ADHD).

- Pupil voice is essential in designing effective nature-based learning that works for all.

- When challenges arise, ensure that communication is clear and pupil choice is central to decision-making.

FINAL THOUGHTS

Sometimes it takes a big shock for us to take stock of the basics. For many, it was the COVID-19 pandemic that highlighted how important nature is for our well-being. In a nationwide survey in the UK, 9 out of 10 people said that nature is crucial to their mental health, with 40% of them also acknowledging that during restrictions they noticed that nature, wildlife, and visiting local green and natural spaces actively supported their well-being.[1] At the same time, there was a call for classes to be moved outdoors to mitigate some of the effects of high contagion of an airborne virus in busy, indoor spaces such as classrooms.[2] And yet, at a time of rapid change, when schools had to adapt to online learning, the call for outdoor learning remained unanswered. Moving forward, I hope we find the energy and motivation to take our pupils outdoors.

We often hear the narrative that children these days have a deficit of experience in relation to the natural world; Richard Louv even wrote a very influential and inspiring book about 'nature-deficit disorder'.[3] The jury is out on whether this generation has experienced this purported 'extinction of experience'[4] and at least one empirical study

---

1   Office for National Statistics, How has lockdown changed our relationship with nature? (26 April 2021). Available at: https://www.ons.gov.uk/economy/ environmentalaccounts/articles/howhaslockdownchangedourrelationship withnature/2021-04-26.

2   J. Quay, T. Gray, G. Thomas, S. Allen-Craig, M. Asfeldt, S. Andkjaer et al., What future/s for outdoor and environmental education in a world that has contended with COVID-19? *Journal of Outdoor and Environmental Education* 23(2) (2020): 93–117.

3   R. Louv, *Last Child in the Woods: Saving our Children from Nature-Deficit Disorder* (Chapel Hill, NC: Algonquin Books, 2008).

4   M. Soga and K. J. Gaston, Extinction of experience: the loss of human–nature interactions, *Frontiers in Ecology and the Environment* 14(2) (2016): 94–101.

has pointed to it being non-existent.[5] Instead of focusing on pathologising our children's childhood, we need to be looking for ways to enhance and enrich them – positive ways to support all pupils to flourish.

What we do know, with a good degree of certainty, is that rich and meaningful nature experiences can have a big, positive effect on how our children develop cognitively, socially, emotionally and physically; these can range from simple everyday moments – planting a seed and watching a flower bloom – to life-changing residentials. Embedding these experiences into the normal flow of school life for all children is key to achieving equity. Nature contact – that is, simply being in natural environments – can help our pupils be more resilient, more physically active and healthier. Nature connection, on the other hand – the feeling of being a part of, rather than apart from the natural world – can enrich their lives in so many ways: improve their mood and feelings of happiness, give meaning and inspire empathy towards the rest of the natural world and motivate children to actively look after their environment.

Looking forward into the following decades of the 21st century, it can help us meet the challenges ahead. As teachers, parents and responsible citizens, we have a duty to give this gift to the next generation. I hope this book inspires many of you to do so, and gives you both the means and motivation to weave nature into your teaching and learning – if you feel it does, please do not hesitate to contact me and let me know!

5   P. Novotný, E. Zimová, A. Mazouchová and A. Šorgo, Are children actually losing contact with nature, or is it that their experiences differ from those of 120 years ago? *Environment and Behavior* 53(9) (2021): 931-952.

APPENDIX 1: WHAT DOES NATURE-BASED EDUCATION ENCOMPASS AT DIFFERENT AGES WITHIN PRIMARY EDUCATION?

Programmes and experiences[1]	Nursery	Ages 4–7	Ages 7–11
Nature nurseries	✓		
Forest school	✓	✓	✓
Nature nurture groups	✓	✓	✓
Nature-based environmental education		✓	✓
Free nature play	✓	✓	✓
Risky play in nature (age appropriate)	✓	✓	✓

---

1   This list is adapted from a list presented by Kuo et al., Do experiences with nature promote learning?

Programmes and experiences[1]	Nursery	Ages 4–7	Ages 7–11
Day trips to natural spaces/nature reserves	✓	✓	✓
Nature-based residentials			✓
School gardens	✓	✓	✓
Wilderness adventures			✓
Indoor nature (plants or animals)	✓	✓	✓
Nature walks (parks, forests, beach)	✓	✓	✓
Beach school	✓	✓	✓
Camp experiences			✓
Animal-assisted learning	✓	✓	✓

APPENDIX 2: RESIDENTIAL PRE- AND POST-VISIT ACTIVITIES

Provide children with a notebook for before, during and after the trip. Ask them to decorate it if they wish – if you have the capacity to take pictures and print them, offer some to stick on the cover or inside their book. Leave the first page blank to be filled in later.

BEFORE THE TRIP

Ask children to consider the following questions, writing the answers in their notebooks:

- What are your three best attributes?
- What are your three biggest challenges?
- How do you feel about going on this residential?
- What are you most worried about?
- What are you most excited about?

DURING THE TRIP

Encourage children to keep a diary of activities each night – this can be completely pupil-led or you can offer a general guide or template for them to follow. If you are able, take photos and videos to use later on.

AFTER THE TRIP

Look back on the initial task and instigate a discussion. This can be aided by the journal the children kept during the trip, but also by photos or videos that you took. Focus the discussion on feelings. Then ask the children to record their answers to the following questions:

- What are your three best attributes?

- What are your three biggest challenges?

- What was the one moment where you were at your best? (for example, overcame a challenge, helped someone out, etc.)

- How did you feel?

CREATING A MOTTO

The final activity can be done as a class or as individuals. It is an important link between the trip and everyday life; you will be coming up with a motto. Explain to the class that a motto is a short phrase chosen to encapsulate the beliefs or ideals of them as an individual or a class. Give them some ideas of mottos, or share the school motto if there is one. Take time to shape your own motto. Remember that blank first page? Here is the place for the children to write their motto and illustrate it.

FOLLOW-UP

A month or so after the trip, revisit their notebooks and have a reflective discussion on the impact the trip has had on them. Is their motto still relevant? What opportunities have they had to use some of their new skills? What opportunities would they like to further practise those skills? Help the children make a plan to flex those new muscles!

APPENDIX 3: INITIAL NEARBY-NATURE AUDIT

HOW TO USE THIS AUDIT

Initially audit the natural spaces that are available to you within the school grounds. Look carefully – there may be places you have not considered yet, or areas that, with small improvements, could be used for more activities. Consider what affordances each space has (see page 81 for more on affordances). Then jot down a few possible activities – this is by no means an exhaustive list, but a few examples of how you can see this particular space linking with your teaching, various areas of the curriculum or other activities. This is a working document and you will come back to it many times.

Once you have considered the spaces within the school grounds, think of adjacent or easily accessible natural spaces beyond the school boundaries. You may find spaces that are close, but also consider moving further away – nature reserves or parks are worth considering too, for example, for day trips or more specialised outings.

WITHIN SCHOOL GROUNDS – AN EXAMPLE AUDIT

Where	What	Affordances	Possible activities	Possibilities for improvement
Back playground	Grassy area	Space Fresh air Increased physical activity	Running PE Quiet activities, e.g. reading	Adding shelter
Front playground	Small tree copse	Loose parts Space Biodiversity	Den building Observing wildlife Free play Quiet time	Clearing Adding seating
Side passage of school	Hedge	Biodiversity Natural screen	Observation Tending Mindfulness	Extend Tend
Front playground	Raised planters	…	…	…

BEYOND SCHOOL GROUNDS – AN EXAMPLE AUDIT

Where	What	Affordances	Possible activities	Risk assessment/ barriers to access
Across the road	Village green	Space Fresh air Autonomy	PE Team building Ball games STEM project work	Crossing road Going beyond boundaries Ball into road
800m	Beach	Space Fresh air Autonomy	PE Team building Ball games STEM work	Consider tide times Crossing road Off-lead dogs

Where	What	Affordances	Possible activities	Risk assessment/ barriers to access
1.5km	Local park	Diverse areas (pond, trees, playground, trim trail) Space Fresh air Loose parts Wildlife	Educational day trip STEM curricular and enquiry work Environmental education	Debris left by other park users (broken bottles, cans, dog poo) Interaction with the community (talking to strangers talk) Going beyond boundaries
11km	Nature reserve	Access to unspoilt nature Wildlife,	Educational day trip STEM curricular learning Environmental education	Need bus for access Child–adult ratio to consider
25km	Botanic gardens	⋮	⋮	⋮

APPENDIX 4: RISK ASSESSMENT CO-CREATION PROCESS AND SHEET

Consider using this with children before heading out for an activity. While in the space, review their answers and do a visual check of the area for any additional dangers.

Activity	Space and equipment	Benefits	Potential risks	Precautions	Any further action required
Whittling	Outdoors with vegetable peelers	Learning to use tools Improved motor skills	Cutting oneself Cutting someone else Splinters from wood	Hold peeler in a certain way Peel away from the body Do not wave peeler around	Ensure a first aid kit containing antiseptic wipes and plasters is available
Rolling down slope	No equipment Back of school	Fun	Hurting oneself when rolling Hitting objects or each other	Take turns to roll down the hill Check hill for stones or branches before rolling	None

APPENDIX 5: WHAT IS CHILD-LED LEARNING?

There is often a misconception on what child-led learning is and what it looks like – especially from those who have not been trained or do not have extensive experience in early childhood, where a lot of the learning is indeed child-led. It is important to acknowledge that child-led learning is not only for early years, but extends across the primary years – if not beyond – and should be encouraged at certain times of the week. Nature-based learning can be ideal for child-led activities. For many, child-led learning means 'let them do what they want' and is basically legitimising lazy teaching. However, in reality, child-led learning involves a lot of hard work on the part of the practitioner, as they try to cultivate curiosity, closely observe the child and curate the environment to meet their needs. They need to:

- **Observe and take note of what they notice:** This may or may not be communicated to the child. If the child is in a state of flow and immersed in an activity, it's best not to disturb. Make a note to discuss later. If the child is seeking shared interest, it's a great time to interact and ask them questions that will move on their learning.

- **Set the structure:** As mentioned in the section on autonomy on page 50, and rather counter-intuitively, a clear structure can allow a child to be truly led by their interests while staying safe. By establishing clear and safe boundaries, the child is able to flourish and lead their own learning.

- **Share in their excitement:** Children will often find and express incredible joy in their play and learning.

Be there to share that excitement – this is key to building strong relationships.

- **Respect their choices:** Follow the child's lead. Children are great at finding the right balance of challenge and competence, so notice the activities they choose and follow their lead.

- **Acknowledge their feelings:** Learning and play can be full of frustration and other big feelings. Acknowledge them when they arise and be with them without judgement. Help younger children to regulate their emotions and make sense of their feelings; for older children, empathy is often the best gift you can give.

- **Curate the environment to meet their needs:** It is empowering for a child to be able to meet their own needs within a context. Ensure they have access to the materials they need instead of having to ask – this includes their drinks and snacks. Teach them how to cater for themselves in age-appropriate ways, allowing them the sense of autonomy that will promote self-confidence.

APPENDIX 6: KEY FINE MOTOR SKILLS AND LOOSE PARTS/ NATURE ACTIVITIES TO PROMOTE WRITING DEVELOPMENT

Fine motor skills necessary for writing	Loose parts/nature activity to promote development
Hand and finger strength	Picking up small objects, e.g. pine cones, sticks, stones, seeds
Hand–eye coordination	Playing with mud
Object manipulation	Hanging from ropes/pulling oneself up
Hand dominance	Using tools such as a hammer or saw
Bilateral integration	Cutting sticks Tying knots
Upper-body strength	Swinging and hanging from ropes or branches Climbing Carrying big sticks or other heavy items Pulling items Digging

REFERENCES

Adverse Childhood Experience (ACE) Support Hub Cymru (2021). *What Works to Prevent Adverse Childhood Experiences (ACEs) at the Community Level?* Available at: https://phwwhocc.co.uk/wp-content/uploads/2022/02/What-Works-to-Prevent-ACEs-at-the-Community-Level.-An-Evidence-Review-Mapping-Exercise-Executive-Summary.pdf.

Aggio, D., Smith, L., Fisher, A. and Hamer, M. (2015). Mothers' perceived proximity to green space is associated with TV viewing time in children: the Growing Up in Scotland study, *Preventive medicine* 70: 46–49.

Ainscow, M., Booth, T., Dyson, A., Farrell, P., Frankham, J., Gallannaugh, F. et al. (2006). *Improving Schools, Developing Inclusion*. London: Routledge.

Aknin, L. B., Hamlin, J. K. and Dunn, E. W. (2012). Giving leads to happiness in young children, *PLoS ONE* 7(6): e39211. DOI:10.1371/journal.pone.0039211.

Alexander, R. J., Doddington, C., Gray, J., Hargreaves, L. and Kershner, R. (eds) (2010). *The Cambridge Primary Review Research Surveys*. London: Routledge.

Barasch, A., Diehl, K., Silverman, J. and Zauberman, G. (2017). Photographic memory: the effects of volitional photo taking on memory for visual and auditory aspects of an experience, *Psychological Science* 28(8): 1056–1066.

Barger, B., Larson, L. R., Ogletree, S., Torquati, J., Rosenberg, S., Gaither, C. J. et al. (2020). Tree canopy coverage predicts lower conduct problem severity in children with ASD, *Journal of Mental Health Research in Intellectual Disabilities* 13: 43–61.

Barrable, A. (2018). The 100 days that changed my life (and how they can change yours too) [video], TEDxLimassol (10 November). Available at: https://www.ted.com/talks/alexia_barrable_the_100_days_that_changed_my_life_and_how_they_can_change_yours_too.

Barrable, A. (2019). Refocusing environmental education in the early years: a brief introduction to a pedagogy for connection, *Education Sciences* 9(1): 61.

Barrable, A. and Arvanitis, A. (2019). Flourishing in the forest: looking at forest school through a self-determination theory lens, *Journal of Outdoor and Environmental Education* 22(1): 39–55.

Barrable, A. and Booth, D. (2020). Green and screen: does mobile photography enhance or hinder our connection to nature?, *Digital Culture & Education* 12(2). Available at: https://static1.squarespace.com/static/5cf15af7a259990001706378/t/5f02e912b96a0625120affc5/1594026261822/Barrable+%26+Booth-merged.pdf.

Barrable, A. and Booth, D. (2020). Increasing nature connection in children: a mini review of interventions, *Frontiers in Psychology* 11: 492.

Barrable, A., Booth, D., Adams, D. and Beauchamp, G. (2021). Enhancing nature connection and positive affect in children through mindful engagement with natural environments, *International Journal of Environmental Research and Public Health* 18(9): 4785.

Baumeister, R. F., Leith, K. P., Muraven, M. and Bratslavsky E. (2002). Self-regulation as a key to success in life. In D. Pushkar, W. M. Bukowski, A. E. Schwartzman, D. M. Stack and D. R. White (eds.), *Improving Competence Across the Lifespan*. Boston, MA: Springer, pp. 117–132.

Beere, J. (2020). *Independent Thinking on Teaching and Learning: Developing Independence and Resilience in All Teachers and Learners*. Carmarthen: Independent Thinking Press.

Beute, F. and De Kort, Y. A. W. (2014). Natural resistance: exposure to nature and self-regulation, mood, and physiology after ego-depletion, *Journal of Environmental* Psychology 40: 167–178.

Bikomeye, J. C., Balza, J. and Beyer, K. M. (2021). The impact of schoolyard greening on children's physical activity and socioemotional health: a systematic review of experimental studies, *International Journal of Environmental Research and Public Health* 18(2): 535.

Bishop, S. R., Lau, M., Shapiro, S., Carlson, L., Anderson, N. D., Carmody, J. et al. (2004). Mindfulness: a proposed operational definition, *Clinical Psychology: Science and Practice* 11(3): 230–241.

Boath, L. and Barrable, A. (2020). The child as co-researcher in the early years: what do children like in the outdoors? *SERA Researching Education Bulletin* 9: 34–38.

Boyer, T. W. (2006). The development of risk-taking: a multi-perspective review, *Developmental Review* 26(3): 291–345.

Bradley, K. and Male, D. (2017). 'Forest School is muddy and I like it': perspectives of young children with autism spectrum disorders, their parents and educational professionals, *Educational and Child Psychology* 34(2): 80–96.

Bridgman, T., Cummings, S. and Ballard, J. (2019). Who built Maslow's pyramid? A history of the creation of management studies' most famous symbol and its implications for management education, *Academy of Management Learning & Education* 18(1): 81–98.

Chan, Y. N., Choy, Y. S., To, W. M. and Lai, T. M. (2021). Influence of classroom soundscape on learning attitude, *International Journal of Instruction* 14(3): 341–358.

Dadvand, P., Nieuwenhuijsen, M. J., Esnaola, M., Forns, J., Basagaña, X., Alvarez-Pedrerol, M. et al. (2015). Green spaces and cognitive development in primary schoolchildren, *Proceedings of the National Academy of Sciences* 112(26): 7937–7942.

Donovan, G., Michael, Y., Gatziolis, D., 't Mannetje, A. and Douwes, J. (2019). Exposure to the natural environment and rurality is protective of ADHD in a large birth cohort of New Zealand children, *Environmental Epidemiology* 3: 103.

Education Endowment Foundation (2019). *Improving Behaviour in Schools: Guidance Report*. Available at: https://educationendowmentfoundation.org.uk/education-evidence/guidance-reports/behaviour.

Engemann, K. Pedersen, C. B., Arge, L., Tsirogiannis, C., Mortensen, P. B. and Svenning, J. C. (2019). Residential green space in childhood is associated with lower risk of psychiatric disorders from adolescence into adulthood, *Proceedings of the National Academy of Sciences* 116(11): 5188–5193.

Escolano-Pérez, E., Herrero-Nivela, M. L. and Losada, J. L. (2020). Association between preschoolers' specific fine (but not gross) motor skills and later academic competencies: educational implications, *Frontiers in Psychology* 11: 1044.

Fägerstam, E. (2014). High school teachers' experience of the educational potential of outdoor teaching and learning, *Journal of Adventure Education & Outdoor Learning* 14(1): 56–81.

Felsten, G. (2009). Where to take a study break on the college campus: an attention restoration theory perspective, *Journal of Environmental Psychology* 29(1): 160–167.

Hansen Sandseter, E. B. (2007). Categorising risky play – how can we identify risk-taking in children's play? *European Early Childhood Education Research Journal* 15(2): 237–252.

Haviland-Jones, J., Rosario, H. H., Wilson, P. and McGuire, T. R. (2005). An environmental approach to positive emotion: flowers, *Evolutionary Psychology* 3(1). DOI.10.1177/147470490500300109

Higashida, N. (2007). *The Reason I Jump*, tr. K. A. Yoshida and D. Mitchell. New York: Penguin Random House.

Hughes, M. and Tucker, W. (2018). Poverty as an adverse childhood experience, *North Carolina Medical Journal* 79(2): 124–126.

Hunter, M. R., Gillespie, B. W. and Chen, S. Y. P. (2019). Urban nature experiences reduce stress in the context of daily life based on salivary biomarkers, *Frontiers in Psychology* 10: 722.

Ikei, H., Song, C. and Miyazaki, Y. (2017). Physiological effects of touching wood, *International Journal of Environmental Research and Public Health* 14(7): 801.

Kapp, S. K., Steward, R., Crane, L., Elliott, D., Elphick, C., Pellicano, E. et al. (2019). 'People should be allowed to do what they like': autistic adults' views and experiences of stimming, *Autism* 23(7): 1782–1792.

Karakasidis, S. (2016). WWF Greece introduces app mapping urban green areas, *Greece Is* (14 June). Available at: https://www.greece-is.com/news/wwf-greece-introduces-app-mapping-urban-green-areas.

Kuo, M., Barnes, M. and Jordan, C. (2019). Do experiences with nature promote learning? Converging evidence of a cause-and-effect relationship, *Frontiers in Psychology* 10: 305.

Kuo, F. E. and Faber Taylor, A. (2004). A potential natural treatment for attention-deficit/hyperactivity disorder: evidence from a national study, *American Journal of Public Health* 94(9): 1580–1586.

Larson, L. R., Barger, B., Ogletree, S., Torquati, J., Rosenberg, S., Gaither, C. J. et al. (2018). Gray space and green space proximity associated with higher anxiety in youth with autism, *Health & Place* 53: 94–102.

Lee, M. S., Lee, J., Park B. J. and Miyazaki, Y. (2015). Interaction with indoor plants may reduce psychological and physiological stress by suppressing autonomic nervous system activity in young adults: a randomized crossover study, *Journal of Physiological Anthropology* 34: 21.

Li, Q. (2010). Effect of forest bathing trips on human immune function, *Environmental Health and Preventive Medicine* 15(1): 9–17.

Lim, C., Donovan, A. M., Harper, N. J. and Naylor, P. J. (2017). Nature elements and fundamental motor skill development opportunities at five elementary school districts in British Columbia, *International Journal of Environmental Research and Public Health* 14(10): 1279.

Louv, R. (2008). *Last Child in the Woods: Saving our Children from Nature-Deficit Disorder*. Chapel Hill, NC: Algonquin Books.

Lumber, R., Richardson, M. and Sheffield, D. (2017). Beyond knowing nature: contact, emotion, compassion, meaning, and beauty are pathways to nature connection, *PLoS ONE* 12(5). DOI:10.1371/journal.pone.0177186.

Lundy, L. (2007). 'Voice' is not enough: conceptualising Article 12 of the United Nations Convention on the Rights of the Child, *British Educational Research Journal* 33(6): 927–942.

Mausner, C. (1996). A kaleidoscope model: defining natural environments, *Journal of Environmental Psychology* 16(4): 335–348.

Merrick, M. T., Ford, D. C., Ports, K. A. and Guinn, A. S. (2018). Prevalence of adverse childhood experiences from the 2011–2014 behavioral risk factor surveillance system in 23 states, *JAMA Pediatrics* 172(11): 1038–1044.

Mirrahimi, S., Tawil, N. M., Abdullah, N. A. G., Surat M. and Usman, I. M. S. (2011). Developing conducive sustainable outdoor learning: the impact of natural environment on learning, social and emotional intelligence, *Procedia Engineering* 20: 389–396.

Mischel, W., Ayduk, O., Berman, M. G., Casey, B. J., Gotlib, I. H., Jonides, J. et al. (2011). 'Willpower' over the life span: decomposing self-regulation, *Social Cognitive and Affective Neuroscience* 6(2): 252–256.

Mochizuki-Kawai, H., Matsuda I. and Mochizuki, S. (2020). Viewing a flower image provides automatic recovery effects after psychological stress, *Journal of Environmental Psychology* 70: 101445.

Nature Friendly Schools (2019). New 'Nature Friendly Schools' will help to 'green' hundreds of school grounds and bring thousands of children closer to nature (1 February). Available at: https://www.naturefriendlyschools.co.uk/new-project-will-help-green-hundreds-school-grounds-and-bring-children-closer-nature.

NHS England (2018). *Delivering Effective Services for Children and Young People with ADHD: Good Practice Guidance for Commissioners and Service Providers across Greater Manchester*. Available at: https://www.england.nhs.uk/north-west/wp-content/uploads/sites/48/2019/03/GM-wide-ADHD-guidance.pdf.

Novotný, P., Zimová, E., Mazouchová A. and Šorgo, A. (2021). Are children actually losing contact with nature, or is it that their experiences differ from those of 120 years ago? *Environment and Behavior* 53(9): 931–952.

Office for National Statistics (2020). One in eight British households has no garden (14 May). Available at: https://www.ons.gov.uk/economy/environmentalaccounts/articles/oneineightbritishhouseholdshasnogarden/2020-05-14.

Office for National Statistics (2021). How has lockdown changed our relationship with nature? (26 April). Available at: https://www.

ons.gov.uk/economy/environmentalaccounts/articles/
howhaslockdownchangedourrelationshipwithnature/2021-04-26.

Ohly, H., Gentry, S., Wigglesworth, R., Bethel, A., Lovell, R. and Garside, R. (2016). A systematic review of the health and well-being impacts of school gardening: synthesis of quantitative and qualitative evidence, *BMC Public Health* 16: 286.

Okada, H., Kuhn, C., Feillet, H. and Bach, J. F. (2010). The 'hygiene hypothesis' for autoimmune and allergic diseases: an update, *Clinical & Experimental Immunology* 160(1): 1–9.

Palagi, E., Burghardt, G. M., Smuts, B., Cordoni, G., Dall'Olio, S., Fouts, H. N. et al. (2016). Rough-and-tumble play as a window on animal communication, *Biological Reviews of the Cambridge Philosophical Society* 91(2): 311–327.

Putra, I. G. N. E., Astell-Burt, T., Cliff, D. P., Vella, S. A., John, E. E. and Feng, X. (2020). The relationship between green space and prosocial behaviour among children and adolescents: a systematic review, *Frontiers in Psychology* 11: 859.

Quay, J., Gray, T., Thomas, G., Allen-Craig, S., Asfeldt, M., Andkjaer S. et al. (2020). What future/s for outdoor and environmental education in a world that has contended with COVID-19? *Journal of Outdoor and Environmental Education* 23(2): 93–117.

Richardson, E. A., Pearce, J., Shortt, N. K. and Mitchell, R. (2017). The role of public and private natural space in children's social, emotional and behavioural development in Scotland: a longitudinal study, *Environmental Research* 158: 729–736.

Richardson, M., Hunt, A., Hinds, J., Bragg, R., Fido, D., Petronzi, D. and White, M. (2019). A measure of nature connectedness for children and adults: validation, performance, and insights, *Sustainability* 11(12): 3250.

Richardson, M. and Sheffield, D. (2017). Three good things in nature: noticing nearby nature brings sustained increases in connection with nature, *PsyEcology* 8(1): 1–32.

Robertson, J. (2017). *Messy Maths: A Playful, Outdoor Approach for Early Years*. Carmarthen: Independent Thinking Press.

Roe, J. and Aspinall, P. (2011). The restorative outcomes of forest school and conventional school in young people with good and poor behaviour, *Urban Forestry & Urban Greening* 10(3): 205–212.

Roffey, S. (2012). Introduction. In S. Roffey (ed), *Positive Relationships: Evidence Based Practice Across the World*. Dordrecht: Springer.

Roslund, M. I., Puhakka, R., Grönroos, M., Nurminen, N., Oikarinen, S., Gazali, A. M. et al. (2020). Biodiversity intervention enhances immune regulation and health-associated commensal microbiota among daycare children, *Science Advances* 6(42): 2578.

Ryan, R. M. and Deci, E. L. (2017). *Self-Determination Theory: Basic Psychological Needs in Motivation, Development, and Wellness*. New York: Guildford Press.

Schutte, A. R., Torquati, J. C. and Beattie, H. L. (2017). Impact of urban nature on executive functioning in early and middle childhood, *Environment and Behavior* 49(1): 3–30.

Scrutton, R. A. (2015). Outdoor adventure education for children in Scotland: quantifying the benefits, *Journal of Adventure Education & Outdoor Learning* 15(2): 123–137.

Sharma-Brymer, V., Brymer, E., Gray, T. and Davids, K. (2018). Affordances guiding forest school practice: the application of the ecological dynamics approach, *Journal of Outdoor and Environmental Education* 21: 103–115.

Shield, B. and Dockrell, J. E. (2004). External and internal noise surveys of London primary schools, *Journal of the Acoustical Society of America* 115(2): 730–738.

Shoda, Y., Mischel, W. and Peake, P. K. (1990). Predicting adolescent cognitive and self-regulatory competencies from preschool delay of gratification: identifying diagnostic conditions, *Developmental Psychology* 26(6): 978.

Soga, M. and Gaston, K. J. (2016). Extinction of experience: the loss of human–nature interactions, *Frontiers in Ecology and the Environment* 14(2): 94–101.

Stefanou, C. R., Perencevich, K. C., DiCintio, M. and Turner, J. C. (2004). Supporting autonomy in the classroom: ways teachers encourage student decision making and ownership, *Educational Psychologist* 39(2): 97–110.

Tandon, P. S., Saelens, B. E., Zhou, C. and Christakis, D. A. (2018). A comparison of preschoolers' physical activity indoors versus outdoors at child care, *International Journal of Environmental Research and Public Health* 15(11): 2463.

Taylor, L., Hahs, A. K. and Hochuli D. F. (2017), Wellbeing and urban living: nurtured by nature, *Urban Ecosystems* 21(1): 197–208.

Touloumakos, A. K. and Barrable, A. (2020). Adverse childhood experiences: the protective and therapeutic potential of nature, *Frontiers in Psychology* 11: 597935.

Ulset, V., Vitaro, F., Brendgen, M., Bekkhus, M. and Borge, A. I. (2017). Time spent outdoors during preschool: links with children's cognitive and behavioral development, *Journal of Environmental Psychology* 52: 69–80.

UNISON (2016). *Bad Form: Behaviour in Schools, UNISON Survey.* Available at: https://www.unison.org.uk/content/uploads/2016/06/Behaviour-in-Schools.pdf.

Van den Bogerd, N., Dijkstra, S. C., Koole, S. L., Seidell, J. C., de Vries, R. and Maas, J. (2020). Nature in the indoor and outdoor study environment and secondary and tertiary education students' well-being, academic outcomes, and possible mediating pathways: a systematic review with recommendations for science and practice, *Health & Place* 66: 102403.

Ward Thompson, C., Aspinall, P., Roe, J., Robertson, L. and Miller, D. (2016). Mitigating stress and supporting health in deprived urban communities: the importance of green space and the social environment, *International Journal of Environmental Research and Public Health* 13: 440.

Watts, T. W., Duncan, G. J. and Quan, H. (2018). Revisiting the marshmallow test: a conceptual replication investigating links between early delay of gratification and later outcomes, *Psychological Science* 29(7): 1159–1177.

Weeland, J., Moens, M. A., Beute, F., Assink, M., Staaks, J. P. and Overbeek, G. (2019). A dose of nature: two three-level meta-analyses of the beneficial effects of exposure to nature on children's self-regulation, *Journal of Environmental Psychology* 65: 101326.

White, M. P., Alcock, I., Grellier, J., Wheeler, B. W., Hartig, T., Warber, S. L. et al. (2019). Spending at least 120 minutes a week in nature is associated with good health and wellbeing, *Scientific Reports* 9: 7730.

Wood, L. A., Tomlinson, M. M., Pfeiffer, J. A., Walker, K. L., Keith, R. J., Smith, T. et al. (2021). Time spent outdoors and sleep normality: a preliminary investigation, *Population Medicine* 3: 7.

Wu, J. and Jackson, L. (2017). Inverse relationship between urban green space and childhood autism in California elementary school districts, *Environment International* 107: 140–146.

Xiong, S., Sankaridurg, P., Naduvilath, T., Zang, J., Zou, H., Zhu, J. et al. (2017). Time spent in outdoor activities in relation to myopia prevention and control: a meta-analysis and systematic review, *Acta Ophthalmologica* 95(6): 551–566.

FURTHER READING

GENERAL

Beere, J. (2020). *Independent Thinking on Teaching and Learning: Developing Independence and Resilience in All Teachers and Learners.* Carmarthen: Independent Thinking Press.

HEALTH AND WELL-BEING

Barrable, A. and Barrable, D. (2017). *Growing Up Wild: 30 Great Ways to Get Your Kids Outdoors.* London: Hachette UK.

PROSOCIAL BEHAVIOURS

Putra, I. G. N. E., Astell-Burt, T., Cliff, D. P., Vella, S. A., John, E. E., and Feng, X. (2020). The relationship between green space and prosocial behaviour among children and adolescents: a systematic review, *Frontiers in Psychology* 11: 859.

POSITIVE RELATIONSHIPS

Roffey, S. (2012). Introduction. In S. Roffey (ed.), *Positive Relationships: Evidence Based Practice Across the World.* Dordrecht: Springer, pp. 1–15.

NATURE CONNECTION IN CHILDREN AND GENERALLY

Finding Nature – https://findingnature.org.uk. An excellent blog by Professor Miles Richardson, one of the world's leading experts on nature connection.

CURRICULAR LEARNING OUTDOORS

Barron, P. (2013). *Games, Ideas and Activities for Primary Outdoor Learning*. London: Pearson Education.

Grandin, T. (2021). *The Outdoor Scientist: The Wonder of Observing the Natural World*. New York: Penguin.

Loxley, P. (2020). *Big Ideas in Outdoor Primary Science: Understanding and Enjoying the Natural World*. Oxon: Routledge.

MacFarlane, C. (2013). *Write Out of the Classroom: How to Use the 'Real' World to Inspire and Create Amazing Writing*. Oxon: Routledge.

Robertson, J. (2014). *Dirty Teaching: A Beginner's Guide to Learning Outdoors*. Carmarthen: Independent Thinking Press.

Robertson, J. (2017). *Messy Maths: A Playful, Outdoor Approach for Early Years*. Carmarthen: Independent Thinking Press.

Sargent, M. (2020). *Developing Early Literacy Skills Outdoors*. London: Practical Pre-School Books.

Selly, P. B. (2017). *Teaching STEM Outdoors: Activities for Young Children*. St Paul, MN: Redleaf Press.

APPS AND OTHER TECHNOLOGY THAT CAN ENHANCE NATURE-BASED LEARNING

Awe – https://www.awe.fyi. An app offering guided meditations to connect to nature.

LeafSnap – https://leafsnap.app. A plant identification app.

Woodland Trust – https://www.woodlandtrust.org.uk/trees-woods-and-wildlife/british-trees/tree-id-app. A tree identification app for the UK.

eGuide to British Birds – https://apps.apple.com/gb/app/eguide-to-british-birds/id508710818. An app to identify British birds.

Text-A-Tree – https://www.halifaxtreeproject.com/textatree. A public engagement project and academic study, undertaken in 2019, testing how technology can help encourage a connection with nature.

(Apps are also available for identifying bugs, butterflies, animal tracks and celestial bodies – even during the day.)

PUPIL VOICE AND PARTICIPATION

Cheminais, R. (2013). *Engaging Pupil Voice to Ensure that Every Child Matters: A Practical Guide*. London: Routledge.

The Lundy model of child participation can be found here: https://ec.europa.eu/info/sites/default/files/lundy_model_of_participation.pdf.

AUTISM

James, M. (2018). *Forest School and Autism: A Practical Guide*. London: Jessica Kingsley Publishers.

Higashida, N. (2013). *The Reason I Jump*, tr. K. A. Yoshida and D. Mitchell. New York: Penguin Random House.

ACES AND TRAUMA-INFORMED PRACTICE

For a full list and more information on ACEs, see https://developingchild.harvard.edu/resources/aces-and-toxic-stress-frequently-asked-questions.

Touloumakos, A. K. and Barrable, A. (2020). Adverse childhood experiences: the protective and therapeutic potential of nature, *Frontiers in Psychology* 11: 597935.

USEFUL ORGANISATIONS

LEARNING THROUGH LANDSCAPES – WWW.LTL.ORG.UK

The biggest UK charity that aims to help children and young people become active, learn outdoors, connect with nature and have fun through outdoor learning and transforming school grounds.

NATURE FRIENDLY SCHOOLS – WWW.NATUREFRIENDLYSCHOOLS.CO.UK

A project that is part of England's 25-year Environment Plan to encourage children to come closer to the natural world in order to support their health and well-being. Nature Friendly Schools work with teachers to increase their confidence in delivering meaningful nature-based experiences.

OUTWARD BOUND TRUST – WWW.OUTWARDBOUND.ORG.UK

An educational charity that aims to help children and young people have adventures in the wilderness that will challenge and change their perspective on life and teach them to believe in themselves and their power to achieve.

INDEPENDENT THINKING ON ...

978-178135337-0

978-178135338-7

978-178135339-4

978-178135340-0

978-178135341-7

978-178135369-1

978-178135373-8

978-178135400-1

978-178135353-0

independent thinking press

www.independentthinkingpress.com

independent thinking

Independent Thinking. An education company.

Taking people's brains for a walk since 1994.

We use our words.

www.independentthinking.com